Live
The Simple Life
You Dream About

*Finding Happiness
Through Refocusing Your Priorities*

Mr. Bobby G. Muse Jr.
© Copyright 2014

Live the Simple Life You Dream About
© 2014 Mr. Bobby G. Muse Jr.

All rights reserved. Printed in the United States of America. No part of this book may be used or reproduced in any manner whatsoever without prior written consent of the author, except as provided by the United States of America copyright law.

Simple Life Publishing
Louisville, KY
www.SimpleLifePublishing.com

ISBN-10: 0615917402
ISBN-13: 9780615917405
LCCN: 2013920881
Simple Life Publishing
Louisville, KY

Simple Life Publishing titles are available at special quantity discounts for sales promotions, corporate events, fundraising, and educational use. For more information, please contact the author at Simple Life Publishing through the website at www.SimpleLifePublishing.com.

"The best way to predict the future is to create it yourself."

Peter Diamandis

Acknowledgments

To my wife and best friend, Mary, who, while always encouraging me to do my best, allowed me to sit for hours on end in front of a computer to follow my dream.

To my family, whose love and understanding has made this book possible.

Contents

Acknowledgments	v
Introduction	ix
What Does Your Perfect Life Look Like?	1
The Benefits of Living a Needs-Based Lifestyle	15
Living a Needs-Based Life	25
Step One: Establishing a Strong Core-Value System	26
Live the Simple Life You Dream About	53
Step Two: Defining Our Priorities	63
Step Three: Establishing Our Financial Means	83
Step Four: Establishing Our Time Means	117
Step Five: Decluttering Our Lives	131
My Hope for You	145

Introduction

Are you happy? Be honest. Are you really happy? Are you living the life you've always dreamed about? When you wake up in the morning, are you so excited about life that you can't wait to jump out of bed to start your day?

If you are like most people, you're probably not overly excited about anything. You're stuck in a rut, drifting aimlessly through life with no goals and very few priorities. You may tell people that you're living the dream, but in reality, you're miserable, unfulfilled, and dreading even getting out of bed.

Worse yet, most of us don't even realize why we are unhappy. A bad job, financial difficulties, a poor relationship, and countless other reasons may rear their ugly heads from time to time, giving us some insight into our reasons for unhappiness, but unless the discontent controls our lives, sadly, most of us can't put a finger on why we are unhappy. As a result, we go through life with an empty feeling in our stomachs, with no clue about why it is there.

This empty feeling can happen to anyone. No one is immune from unhappiness or the empty feeling we sometimes feel in our stomachs. The feeling doesn't happen only to those of us who are, at the time, reevaluating our lives and looking for more from the lives we live. It also happens to people who seem to be on top of the world and have everything going for them. To us, these people seem to have great jobs, all the money they need, and relationships that are so positive others envy them. But don't be fooled;

some of these same people still feel empty inside and unhappy with their lives and the direction they are taking.

How can people who seem to have everything going for them still be unhappy, still feel empty inside? The main reason most of us feel empty inside is that we have never spent the time or made the effort to define what happiness means to us.

Happiness means different things to different people. Just because something makes one person happy doesn't mean it will make another person feel the same way. Happiness is a deeply personal thing. Someone else cannot tell us what will make us happy, nor can we tell others what will make their empty feeling go away. Individuals must discover for themselves what makes them happy and gives meaning to their lives.

How do we let ourselves get into this dilemma? It's simple. We live our lives haphazardly. Instead of putting forth the time and effort needed to define the lifestyle that will bring us the contentment we are looking for, we muddle along hoping that one day we land on the thing or things that will bring us happiness.

Most often, we fall into the lifestyle we end up living. Instead of fighting for the lifestyle that will bring us the real happiness we're looking for, we let the lifestyle that we sometimes accidently fall into control our destiny.

Don't be mistaken; happiness is very difficult to find through trial and error. Real happiness comes through thoughtful evaluation of our lives and incorporating the things that bring us happiness and meaning into the way we live our lives. Once we make the time to appraise our lives and take the necessary steps to surround ourselves with the people, activities, and things that give us meaning, happiness quickly follows, and the emptiness we feel in our stomachs goes away.

What keeps us from defining the lifestyle we want to live? Like most things in life, getting started—putting one foot in front of the other—holds us back. Although we're unhappy with the lives we're living, for whatever reason, we sometimes lack the motivation necessary to take the steps to eliminate the emptiness we feel. As a result, most of us limp through life thinking that life is as good as it gets, and nothing can be done to make it better—so why even try? This is what I mean by letting the lifestyle we sometimes fall into define our destiny.

I'm not going to lie to you; living your life in a way that gives it meaning is not always easy. It takes time, much self-reflection, and a commitment to focus your life on the things that are important to you. The happiness and contentment it takes to remove the empty feeling in your stomach can't be given to you by someone else, nor can you go to a local store and buy it. You can't sit back in your easy chair and hope it falls into your lap one day. Living a lifestyle that gives your life meaning and satisfaction must be carefully planned for and fought for daily. The life that will fulfill your dreams is out there waiting for you to define it. You must reach out and grab that life and make it your way of living. Why don't you start right now?

There are five major steps we must take to define the lifestyle that will bring us happiness. First, we must reduce or eliminate outside influences on our decision making. We must learn to listen to the voice that comes from within our hearts and use it to make the choices we need to make about how we live our lives. This step is important to helping us understand what we really need to be happy.

Second, we must define our priorities. We must identify the people, activities, and things that are important to us, that bring satisfaction and meaning to our lives. Once we define our priorities, we must stay close to them. We must incorporate them into the very fabric of our lives. At the same time we define our priorities, we must ascertain where we are at this point in our lives and determine where we want our lives to go in the future. We must define and establish tangible goals we can commit to and work toward.

Third, we must develop a solid money-management plan. Living within our means is one of the most important factors determining our happiness. Keeping our spending under control helps keep us on track and removes many of the daily distractions that challenge our efforts at living the lives we want to live. It also allows us to reallocate our funds to support our priorities and goals in a more meaningful way.

Just as we need to develop a solid money-management plan, fourth, we also need to establish a plan to manage our time more efficiently. We have only twenty-four hours a day to live our lives. Once these twenty-four hours are spent, they can never be recovered. They are gone forever. With this plan, we evaluate our time needs and identify places we can reallocate our resources to ensure we spend them on the people, activities, things, and goals that are important to us.

Fifth and finally, we must declutter our lives. We must remove all of the distractions—both physical and emotional—from our lives that keep us from our priorities. These distractions, if we allow them to control us, will suck the life out of us and prevent us from living the lives we dream about. We must take constructive steps to eliminate these distractions from our lives to free up resources—both money and time—that can be used to support our priorities and goals.

Taking these five simple steps will change your life forever. Just as it did with me, maybe for the first time you will understand where you went wrong, and you will have concrete, practical steps to take to get your life back on track. Anyone can say he or she is happy. Anyone can say he or she is living the dream. But to be truly happy, you must first determine what gives meaning to your life. Next, you must develop a plan incorporating all the things that are important to you into your lifestyle with the resources needed to support them. Finally, you must eliminate the clutter that sometimes gets in the way of living the life you dream about. Doing anything else only keeps you on the same path you are on now: living life haphazardly.

Once you take these steps, you will never live haphazardly again. No longer will you hope happiness falls into your lap. You will know what makes you happy, and you will have a proven plan to keep all the people, activities, and things that give your life meaning close to you. Your life will have direction like it's never had before, and the goals you've dreamed about will become an integral part of your life's journey.

A wonderful byproduct of going through this five-step process is that it also allows us to simplify our lives. Carefully defining our priorities and creating plans to keep them as a central focus of our lives allows us to eliminate many of the distractions that make our lives so complicated. Knowing what gives our lives meaning and being able to focus on these things exclusively eliminates most if not all of the trial and error activity that used to dominate our time and energy. With all these things eliminated, life naturally becomes simpler.

If you've read my first book, *The Building Blocks of Success: Focus On the Fundamentals and Be Successful at Everything You Do*, or any of my blogs, you know that I think life is too complicated. I believe that anything that simplifies our lives is worth pursuing. The simpler anything is, the easier it is to accomplish and achieve.

To be clear, however, living a simple life means different things to different people. At one end of the spectrum, living a simple life means going back to an eighteenth-century, horse-and-buggy lifestyle. This manifestation of the simple life is based on a primitive way of life that is sometimes characterized by not having electricity, running water, or modern conveniences. People who live this form of the simple life are mostly interested in total self-sufficiency with little or no reliance on anyone else for their basic needs. I don't know about you, but this doesn't seem like a simple life at all.

On the other end of the spectrum, to some people the simple life may only mean growing vegetables in the family's garden. This characterization of the simple life is not primitive at all and has no goal of ever becoming self-sufficient. It's a lifestyle based on an idea of saving a little money here and there and slowing life down wherever possible. I compare this definition of the simple life to someone sticking their toe into the swimming pool to see if the water is cold before they jump in and get wet. In this definition, there is a limit to what is acceptable and what is reasonably inconvenient.

When I define what the simple life means to me, neither extreme as I have portrayed above is what I am talking about. Living the simple life to me isn't based on an eighteenth-century existence or growing tomatoes in the backyard. Living the simple life in my definition is a way of life based on simplifying our lives through refocusing our energy, time, and resources to the priorities in our lives. Priorities in this case are the people, activities, or things that matter the most to us and ultimately bring happiness to our existence. Although the choices we make eventually define a lifestyle fashioned by our priorities, the definition of the simple life to me is not a lifestyle based on a preconceived way of life we must conform to. The simple life is defined by the priorities we pick and deliberately choose to focus on.

In the context of this book, my definition of the simple life is a state of uncomplicated, straightforward, unpretentious living, unaffected by worldly desires, wants, or standards, where the focus of our lives is based on our priorities, and the value of our lives is measured by our quality of life, not quantity of life. For all our discussions about the simple life, this is my definition.

Now that I have given you my definition of the simple life, how does this measure up against the life you are living? Are you living a simple life? Are you living your life in an uncomplicated manner? Are you living your life in a way that is not influenced by the wants and desires of others? Is your life focused on your priorities—the important people, activities, and things in your life? Do you measure your life's value by the quality of life you enjoy? If you're like most people in our hectic society, you're probably not living a simple life. Like most of us, you're treading water as fast as you can, barely keeping your head above water.

Why do we live this way? Instead of making a conscious effort to focus on the important things in our lives and eliminate the things from our lives that don't measure up, we keep moving as fast as we can, trying to fit everything we possibly can into our lives. We act like a juggler at the circus trying to keep multiple balls in the air, not focusing on any one ball too long, but moving as fast as we can to keep them from hitting the ground. Friends, it's time to slow down, let a few balls drop from our focus, and redirect our lives to what's really important.

Living the simple life helps you focus your time, energy, and resources on the important things in life, the priorities that are important to you. Once you make the commitment to focus on your priorities and reallocate your resources, your life is never the same. Life is simpler. True happiness comes to you naturally.

Do you want to live the simple life as I have described? Do you want to eliminate the clutter in your life and focus on the things that really matter and give meaning to your life?

In the framework of this book, I will discuss the simple life in more detail. You and I will explore the idea of living the simple life, help you start identifying and focusing on your priorities, redirect your resources to the things that are really important to you, and eliminate the clutter that most often gets in the way.

This book is based on my personal journey to find happiness and meaning in my life. Although I am blessed with a beautiful, loving wife, two unbelievably smart and healthy kids, several great jobs over the years, supportive parents, and everything anyone could ask for, deep inside I still wasn't happy. Something was missing in my life. Even though I had every reason to be content, I wasn't.

Out of sheer desperation, I decided to do something about it. I decided to take the advice I had given to countless others throughout the years, and I examined my life and made changes where necessary. For years I told others that "life is too short, and if you are not happy, it is time to do something about it." "Don't waste your life living in a way that doesn't make you happy," I said. So one day in the depths of my despair, I took my own advice. The result of my journey to find happiness and contentment in my life is outlined in this book. I hope you will take advantage of my struggles and my time of soul searching; above all, I hope this book will help you find happiness and meaning in your life.

What Does Your Perfect Life Look Like?

When most people think about their perfect life, they dream about wealth and fame. We see ourselves living in a palatial home somewhere on a tropical island or surrounded by thousands of acres of land. We imagine servants—cooks, butlers, housekeepers, gardeners, chauffeurs, or pool boys—tending to our every need. We dream of having a bank balance so large that the enormity of our wealth makes Bill Gates seem like a homeless person.

When it comes to fame, we're not much better. We want everyone to recognize us when we walk down the street. We want to be on all the talk shows and on the front cover of every magazine. When we speak, we want everyone to crowd around us to listen. When we stand to leave the room, we want everyone to stop and wave good-bye.

Be realistic, do we really want this? Having a lot of money is nice, and it allows us to do things we wouldn't be able to do otherwise, but money doesn't always bring happiness. I've been fortunate throughout my career to work with many very wealthy people. Believe it or not, many of them are not as happy as you would think. Like everyone else, they have problems that make them question who they are and the direction their lives are going. Money alone never buys happiness.

Fame is no different. Once everyone starts focusing on us, we lose our freedom. We can't go anywhere with a friend without someone interrupting our private conversation, asking us for a picture that gets posted to the Internet, or scrutinizing everything we do. It may be fun in the beginning, and it may give us a feeling of extreme self-worth, but shortly after it starts, we wish we could go back to the life we had before we were famous. Fame alone—like money—never brings the happiness to our lives we thought it would bring.

Consider for a moment a life not driven by materialism, but one based on need. Forget wealth and fame for a few minutes and ask yourself, what would it take to make me happy? To say it another way, what is the bare minimum that I require to be happy? Sure lots of money and recognition would be grand, but if you look at life from strictly a needs perspective, what would it really take for you to be happy?

Here's why I ask. When you stop and think about it, we don't really own anything in this life. We're born into this world with nothing, and, when the time comes, we leave this place the same way, with nothing. We only borrow the things we acquire in our life for a short while and then give them to someone else when we die. In time, that person gives our things—their things—to someone else. Having all the money and fame in the universe will not stop this inevitable process from running its course.

So, if all the things we spend our money acquiring we really never own, why do we waste so much of our time and effort attaining things that, in a few short years, will belong to someone else? Do these things play such an important role in our lives that they represent our purpose for living? Are these possessions essential to our happiness? I don't think they are.

Worse yet, we do crazy things to increase our chances of getting the things we want badly. We sometimes work in jobs we hate. We spend extended time away from home and neglect our loved ones to make an extra buck or two. We overextend ourselves in terms of time and money on things that have little to nothing to do with our happiness. Are the crazy things we are doing all of this for essential to our happiness? If they're not, why are we doing them? Why are we not spending our time and resources on the things that really matter to us?

What does your perfect life look like? Who are the people you want to have a major role in your life? What are the priorities in your life that are important to your well-being? What are the "things" that are essential to your happiness? Until you define what your perfect life looks like, you won't know if you are living it.

The first step to living a simple life is living a life based on our needs, not wants. Each of us must answer the question, what will it really take to make me happy? It's important that we define our real needs because focusing on these needs is crucial to making good decisions in all parts of our lives. Allowing outside influences to shift our focus to unrealistic wants affects our decision-making ability, makes us lose focus on our priorities, and causes us to spend our limited resources unnecessarily. Staying focused and living our lives based on our real needs is essential and is the first step in living a simple life.

What are the outside influences I am talking about? Everyone in our society is trying to influence how we spend our time and money, our resources. Buy this, buy that, go here, go there, do this, do that; we're bombarded every day by people with messages that suggest our lives cannot be complete until we buy into their way of thinking. For example, how many times has someone suggested to us that if we don't drive a particular model of car, live in a certain part of town, or dress in a predefined way, people will think less of us? How often has someone tried to convince us that an idea, behavior, or product is better than the one we possess? The overriding purpose of these messages is to influence how we think and use our resources.

Over time, if we buy into these messages, they cloud our thinking and cause us to lose sight of our priorities. Instead of focusing on our real needs and how they relate to the important things in our lives, we allow these messages—if left unchecked—to encourage us to replace our actual needs with unrealistic wants. Once we consider using our resources on unrealistic wants, we start making bad decisions that directly affect our ability to support our priorities. Without focused priorities supported by our resources, it is impossible to live a simple life.

Unrealistic wants have distorted the truth and influenced the decisions of humankind since the beginning of time. As soon as God put man on earth, unrealistic wants became part of his life. The first recorded account happened in the Garden of Eden when God gave Adam and Eve everything except the Tree of Knowledge in the center of the garden.[1] They were instructed to resist the temptation to eat the fruit and were warned that there would be dire consequences if they did. Of course, Eve wouldn't be denied the fruit and convinced Adam that they must eat from the forbidden tree. You know the rest of the story. Adam and Eve ate from the Tree of Knowledge, and God banned them from the Garden of Eden.

Why did they eat from the Tree of Knowledge when God specifically told them not to? The influence of unrealistic wants made them do it. I'm sure there were plenty of other trees in the garden that would satisfy their hunger. Why wouldn't they just leave that tree alone and eat from another tree? Why, because unrealistic wants were at work in Eve's heart, and she wouldn't be happy or satisfied until she and Adam ate from the tree.

Unrealistic wants are that way. They make us think and act in ways we never thought we would even consider, much less act upon. They will sometimes make us take needless risks that affect not only us, but everyone around us, negatively. Unrealistic wants will sometimes make us lie, cheat, or even steal from others to fulfill a desire. They cloud our thinking, decision making, and view of the world.

Adam and Eve may have been the first to experience the power of unrealistic wants, but the destructive power of its influence has been documented throughout history. Now, it is not the purpose of the book to give you a detailed history of world events and how they were affected by the influence of unrealistic wants. However, I do think it is important for us to understand how this powerful influence has no limits on the events it can and has affected. For those of you who are not history buffs, please stay with me through the next several pages as I use history to illustrate the powerful influence that unrealistic wants has on our world, our country, and us. It's only when we understand the historical significance that unrealistic wants have on humankind that we fully understand the importance of eliminating this powerful influence from our lives so we can find true happiness.

Brief Synopsis of Unrealistic Wants on History

The influence of unrealistic wants played a major role in the fall of the Roman Empire. Although there have been many reasons suggested as the rationale for the collapse—political corruption, economic problems, disease, and other warring nations—a series of leaders who were more interested in their own personal gain than the welfare of their common people was the major driving force.[2] Gaius (better known as Caligula), Claudius, and

Nero rained havoc on the empire through their viciousness, arrogance, and inexperience.[3]

Many historians believe that because of the insatiable desire to acquire new sources of revenue, the empire was required to expand further than it had the means to control or protect. Rome, under these three men's leadership, did both. To increase the revenue of their empire and hence their own personal wealth, they increased their tax base by conquering other nations. Unfortunately, by expanding their empire, they lost the ability to protect it, and other nations began to take control of their lands. Because of the influence that was placed on this group of leaders by unrealistic wants and the resulting actions they took, the empire collapsed in 476 AD, ending an era of a highly advanced civilization.

In addition to the fall of great civilizations, the influence of unrealistic wants has played a major role in most, if not all, military conflicts. The American Revolution is a good example of this influence and the misuse of power that led to the independence of thirteen American colonies.[4]

After the French and Indian War, Great Britain was deeply in debt. To raise money, Great Britain imposed several new taxes, including the Sugar Act, Stamp Act, Townshend Act, and the Tea Act. In addition, the British East India Company, a large commodities trading business, was failing. To prop up the company and keep it from going belly-up, the king gave it a monopoly on the tea trade in America.

The colonists were outraged, and, in 1773, in open defiance of Britain's rule, a group of them disguised as Indians dumped tea overboard from three ships in Boston Harbor. Two years later, the American Revolution began, and it led to the independence of the American colonies from Great Britain. Because of Britain's love of money and its need to control the colonies in such a way that benefited only the crown, the colonists rebelled, and Britain lost thirteen American colonies that later became the United States of America, the strongest nation in the modern world.

A significant reason for the Civil War was based on the influence of unrealistic wants. Because of Eli Whitney's invention of the cotton gin in 1793 and the productivity gains that resulted, growing cotton became very profitable.[5] As a result, more and more plantations dropped their other crops in favor of growing cotton. The need for cheap labor—i.e. slaves—was needed to keep up with the upsurge in production. Slaves were essential to sustaining the productivity and profitability of the plantations.

Once Abraham Lincoln, who was viewed as antislavery, was elected President, the proverbial handwriting was on the wall, and the plantation states began to secede from the Union. As a direct result, the Civil War began in 1861 and ended in 1865 with the freeing of the slaves. Because of a strong desire centered in unrealistic wants to maintain cheap labor, 750,000 men lost their lives, and an entire nation was reshaped.[6]

Although these two examples represent significant times in American history, every war or military action fought anywhere in the world throughout the history of mankind has been directly or indirectly influenced by unrealistic wants—the selfish desire to acquire more than one needs. World War I, World War II, the Korean War, the Vietnam War, and the Iraq conflict, just to name a few of the American military confrontations, were the result of this influence.

However, the influence of unrealistic wants is not just limited to wars or military conflicts. It has also influenced financial and money matters throughout history. Perhaps the best known is the stock market crash of 1929—one of the causes of the Great Depression.[7] Investors taking speculative approaches overvalued stock prices and created a frenzy of buying and selling, so much so that the market exchange could not keep up, and, at one point, the ticker-tape machines were running several hours behind.[8] The panic selling left no one willing to buy stocks, and the market had no place to go but down. By October 29, 1929, commonly referred to as "Black Tuesday," the market had fallen 23 percent in two days, and by July of 1932, the market had lost almost 90 percent of its value. It would take twenty-five years before the market fully recovered to its 1929 peak value.[9]

More recently in 2009, Bernard Madoff, a former stockbroker, investment adviser, and the admitted operator of what has been described as the largest Ponzi scheme in history, pleaded guilty to eleven federal crimes. He admitted to turning his wealth-management business into a massive Ponzi scheme that defrauded thousands of investors of billions of dollars.[10] The amount missing from client accounts was reported at around 65 billion dollars.[11] Madoff was sentenced to 150 years in prison for his crimes.

Accounting scandals such as Enron is another example. Enron, a world leading electricity and natural gas company at the time, was accused of hiding company debts and inflating profits by more than one billion dollars.[12] In addition, the company was accused of allegedly offering bribes to foreign governments to win contracts abroad.

In November 2001, Enron, one of the ten largest companies in America, collapsed when a rival company backed out of a deal to purchase it.[13] The influence of unrealistic wants enticed the leadership of Enron to "cook the books" and hide the real truth from the American public, their employees, and their investors.

More recently, the financial crisis starting in 2007 that continues to plague us today was allegedly triggered by a liquidity crisis in the United States banking system.[14] It is considered by many economists to be the worst financial crisis since the Great Depression of the 1930s.[15]

There are two basic reasons for this economic downturn, according to experts. First, borrowers were tempted to borrow more money than they could afford. Second, lenders were enticed to lend money to borrowers who would not normally qualify. In the big picture view of things, this is fairly normal behavior for borrowers. However, in this case, the activity between the borrowers and lenders was facilitated by the lending industry creating risky loan instruments. When the borrowers began to default on their loans, the economy began to spiral out of control. In the end, both borrowers and lenders were driven by the influence of unrealistic wants, which some would say contributed to the failure of key businesses, the decline in consumer wealth estimated in the trillions of dollars, financial bailouts by various governments, and a significant decline in economic activity.[16]

Just as the influence of unrealistic wants has affected financial and money matters, it has also affected environmental disasters. For nearly forty years, corporate giant Monsanto routinely dumped toxic PCB waste into Snow Creek in Anniston, Alabama.[17] According to reports, Monsanto knew exactly how dangerous PCBs were, but decided not to warn the community. Instead, the company allegedly tried to manipulate the results of studies conducted on rats, chickens, and dogs to downplay the toxicity of its product.[18] The company had a monopoly on the PCB market for four decades until the chemical was banned in 1979. Unfortunately, the community of Anniston, Alabama, will continue to feel its effects for many years to come. Monsanto agreed to pay 700 million dollars to clean up the site.

More recently, the BP Deepwater Horizon oil spill purportedly released millions of gallons of oil into the Gulf of Mexico.[19] At the time of the accident, according to news reports, BP was putting extreme pressure on the drilling crew to complete the project. The drilling project was running behind schedule and costing BP millions of dollars a week. A few weeks before the explosion, the blowout preventer, which prevents such disasters from happening, was damaged, and, instead of stopping to properly repair the equipment, the crew pushed on with the accelerated schedule. Even on the day of the explosion, it is reported that BP argued with Transocean, the operator of the well, for a less-costly well-capping shortcut that would allow BP to restart the well much sooner. Shortly afterward, a huge explosion and fire engulfed the drilling platform. Eleven people died on the oil rig and created the largest oil spill in American history.

The influence of unrealistic wants has also influenced the outcome of every type of sporting event. The Black Sox scandal of 1919, perhaps the most well-known, eventually resulted in the ban of eight players for fixing the outcome of the World Series that year.[20]

It also influenced the 1951 point-shaving scandal in which thirty-five active and former college players were accused of fixing basketball games. Between 1947 and 1951, it was alleged that at least eighty-six games were fixed. Perhaps the most famous people involved in the investigation were Alex Groza and Ralph Beard of Adolph Rupp's "Fabulous Five" team at Kentucky that won back-to-back NCAA titles in 1948 and 1949. Because of the scandal, Rupp's team, which won the 1951 NCAA title, had the honor of becoming the first college basketball team to get the "death penalty" and was barred from play in the 1952–53 season. In all, the investigation led to the conviction of twenty players.[21]

The influence of unrealistic wants convinced Pete Rose that it was okay to bet on baseball games. His decision ended up costing him not only a sure place in baseball's Hall of Fame, but also a long managing career. Rose, who was called "Mr. Hustle" during his playing days, had been the Reds' skipper from 1984 until he was banned from baseball in 1989.[22]

More recently, in 2010, Saint Louis Cardinal Mark McGwire admitted to steroid use after many years of denying numerous reports from teammates, friends, and the media. He is credited with 583 home runs, including the record-hitting season of 70 homers in 1998.[23] McGwire is now the fourth player in the top twenty all-time Major League Baseball home-run hitters linked to the use of performance-enhancing drugs.[24]

But the influence of unrealistic wants doesn't affect only the fall of great civilizations, wars and military conflicts, financial and money matters, environmental disasters, and sporting events. Even Christian evangelists and men of God are not immune from the powerful influence that unrealistic wants puts on them. Kent Hovind, an American Baptist minister and Young Earth creationist, was convicted of fifty-eight federal tax offenses and related charges, for which he was given a ten-year sentence.[25] Richard Roberts, former president of Oral Roberts University and son of the late televangelist Oral Roberts, was named as a defendant in a lawsuit alleging improper use of university funds for political and personal purposes.[26] In fact, the problem of Christian evangelists improperly using church funds seemed so prevalent in 2007 that Senator Chuck Grassley (R-IA) opened a three-year probe into the finances of six televangelists to investigate reports of lavish lifestyles paid for by their television viewers who donated to their ministries.[27] These ministers reportedly had extravagant mansions, private jets, and other expensive items allegedly bought with donated monies.

In short, unrealistic wants have influenced behavior in every civilization, culture, and nationality throughout history. They have determined strategies in every war, conflict, and police action throughout the world. Unrealistic wants have created scandal in companies in all types of industries. They have created and determined the outcomes of environmental disasters everywhere. They have influenced the outcome of all types of sporting events, games of chance, and friendly competitions. Unrealistic wants have ruined the lives of godly people in every denomination, religion, and faith. We could dedicate an entire book to reviewing the history of unrealistic wants and all the times it has influenced or changed the direction of the world. However, the history of the influence of unrealistic wants is not the purpose of this book.

The main idea behind the brief review of history just presented is that unrealistic wants, at some point, touch every person, place, or thing known to man. More importantly, everything that the influence of unrealistic wants touches, changes in ways that cannot always be expected or anticipated. And sometimes, despite our best efforts, the influence of unrealistic wants appears in the form of evil and destroys everything with which it comes in contact.

Not only has the influence of unrealistic wants shown its ugly head throughout the history of mankind, it continues to influence our behavior in every individual decision we make today. Every day we are bombarded with messages, subtle and unsubtle, directed at our unrealistic wants gene about how we should think and live our lives. For example, politicians on a regular basis suggest to us how we should think and vote on certain issues.

They say, "Vote for me because I am just like you. I know what you want and need, and if you elect me, I will make sure you get it." But it rarely happens. Why? Because the influence of unrealistic wants interferes with their once-good intentions and skews their decision-making process. When this happens, their priorities change, and their political ideologies become more important than the people they were sent to serve.

Companies selling products and services through advertising strive to assure us that to be happy, we have to drive a certain car, live in a certain part of town, or dress in a certain way. By the end of the advertisement, their goal is to have us convinced that we must have whatever they are selling.

The entertainment industry provides twenty-four-hour programming that entertains us with lifestyles of how other people—real and fictional—live their lives. Over time, it is only natural for us to question how we live our lives and compare our lives against those we see in movies and television.

If we let it happen, eventually these messages and others like them mold and shape who we are, how we think, and how we respond to life's daily events. More importantly, they sometimes influence how we live our lives and directly sway the decisions we make. In the end, these messages can affect our behavior, happiness, and life goals. If they remain unchecked, they can bring about a change in our way of life—a lifestyle not determined by us, but chosen as the result of the influence of unrealistic wants communicated to us by others.

All of the messages we are inundated with are almost always prejudiced by unrealistic wants. Each message attempts to sell us a way of life, a way of thinking, or a belief we should embrace. In the examples above, the politician is driven to get elected and acquire the position and power that comes with an elected office. Unrealistic wants sometimes drive him or her to satisfy party leaders or donors and vote in ways that may be contrary to the way they or their constituents personally believe.

Unrealistic wants drive corporate America to persuade us to buy products or services to increase its bottom-line profits. Its main goal is to make money, lots of money. As history has shown, if the leaders of these organizations don't reach their financial goals, they are sometimes motivated by unrealistic wants to do despicable things to increase their profit margins.

The entertainment industry is driven by unrealistic wants to control the market share of its industry and increase the advertising rates it can charge their customers. The higher the rates, the more money the industry stands to earn, the happier its investors will be, and the easier it will be to secure funds for new projects. To achieve the market share demanded, industry leaders sometimes let unrealistic wants persuade them to present messages that are not representative of societal norms or standards, but rather present messages that test the standards of decency. In almost every case, the message is defined by unrealistic wants to meet the wants and desires of the messenger.

Although the love of money and power drives the messages in the examples above, our own unrealistic wants influence the decisions we make. We allow unrealistic wants to influence how we think and let them sway our decisions. Let's face it: politicians, corporate America, and the entertainment industry try to influence us by using to their advantage what they already know about us—that we are greedy by nature. As a result, they craft their messages to take advantage of this knowledge about us, and it is used to influence our behavior.

When we make a decision, we rarely make a decision that is not influenced by unrealistic wants. For example, the car we drive is influenced by unrealistic wants. Any well-maintained car will get us from point A to point B. However, the desire of getting from point A to point B is not what typically determines our purchasing decision. Most of us let unrealistic wants persuade us into believing that we need a good-looking car with all the bells and whistles. We don't want a plain car. We want luxury items such as leather seats, satellite radio, dual-control air conditioning, moon roof, backup camera, and automatic parallel parking, just to name a few. Would a car with rust on the hood, vinyl seats, and an AM radio get us to where we want to go? Sure it would, but the influence of unrealistic wants tells us that this is not the kind of car we want to be seen driving.

Most of us cannot afford the car of our dreams, but we still let the influence of our unrealistic wants determine what we purchase. As a result, we sometimes spend more than we should to get as close to our dream car as possible. We reason, "I work hard and deserve all the bells and whistles." "Everybody I know has leather seats in their car. Why shouldn't I have them too?" "What would my friends and coworkers think if they saw me driving an old rusted car?" we might ask. As you can see, more times than not the influence of unrealistic wants has a direct impact on the car we ultimately purchase.

What about the television you watch every day? Do you have the latest big-screen, flat-panel 3D television? I'm dating myself here, but remember the days of black-and-white television? When the best quality picture was made up of 264 shades of gray?

When the color television came on the market, everybody had to have one. Why? Did the black-and-white television not work anymore? No, it worked fine. So what made the color television better? Color was presented to us by advertisers as being superior to black and white. Who wanted to watch anything in black and white if you could watch it in deep, rich color? Never mind the fact that most television shows weren't even produced in color for many years after the color television was introduced. Unrealistic wants made us throw out the old black-and-white TV and purchase a new color set.

How was your drive into work this morning? Was the traffic heavy and causing long lines and backups? Did someone try to avoid the delay and blink his or her way into the line in front of you? Sure he did. The influence of unrealistic wants made him do it. In his mind, his time is more valuable than yours, and he didn't have time to wait like everyone else. He reasoned to himself that you wouldn't mind him cutting in front of you. As the result of this kind of behavior, road-rage has increased tremendously in the last several years, and it has led to numerous car accidents, lawsuits, and even murder.

Not until we stop and look at history and understand how the influence of unrealistic wants directly affects our lives, can we change our behavior, stop the influence it has on us, and simplify our lives. Reducing the influence unrealistic wants has on our lives allows us find happiness as we refocus our priorities.

Suffice it to say that living a life based on unrealistic wants has influenced negative behavior in every civilization, culture, and nationality. It has driven strategies in every war, conflict, and police action throughout the world. It has created scandal in companies in all types of industry. It has created, influenced, and determined the outcome of every environmental disaster. It has influenced the results of sporting events, games of chance, and friendly competitions. Most shocking, perhaps, living a life based on unrealistic wants has ruined the lives of godly people in every denomination, religion, and faith.

Not surprisingly, living a life based on unrealistic wants is the ultimate motivator. This way of thinking is one of, if not the most powerful and destructive influences known to man. According to the *Encarta Dictionary*, it is the desire to acquire more than one needs to the detriment of everything else. This kind of thinking directly influences our view of the world and confuses our life's priorities.

In addition, living a life based on unrealistic wants has no boundaries. If allowed to manifest, it will influence every part of our lives. Moreover, living our lives this way can not only devastate individuals and families, but it has also been known to destroy countries and entire civilizations.

Once this way of thinking takes hold of our lives, can we ever be satisfied? Honestly, it is very difficult. It is almost impossible to satisfy unrealistic wants because unrealistic wants breed more unrealistic wants. Once we fulfill one desire, a new desire is created.

Worse yet, if a life built on unrealistic wants can never be satisfied, it will be difficult, if not impossible, to find real happiness. Happiness is the direct result of being satisfied, satisfied with who we are, what we are doing, and where our lives are going. Being satisfied is a prerequisite of happiness. If we can't be satisfied, how can we be happy? Vernon Howard, an American author, said it best: "You have succeeded in life when all you really want is only what you really need."[28]

Are you living a life based on unrealistic wants? Are you letting unrealistic wants get in the way of your priorities? Are you spending your resources unnecessarily trying to satisfy these wants? To live the simple life and find the true happiness that comes from this lifestyle, you must base your life on your real needs to free up resources to support your life's priorities.

Next, we will discuss the benefits of living a life based on real needs and how it contributes to focusing on our priorities.

The Benefits of Living a Needs-Based Lifestyle

When we stop living our lives based on unrealistic wants, by default, our satisfaction goes up, and our lives get simpler. No longer are we influenced by messages that can confuse our thinking and compete for our resources. We are able to isolate ourselves from outside influences and determine how we want to live our lives based on our own personal values and priorities.

Living a needs-based lifestyle provides five benefits. First, our decision-making process becomes much clearer. Unrealistic wants have a tendency to cloud our thinking by allowing needs to become unrealistic wants. Focusing directly on our real needs helps us to identify unnecessary wants quickly and keeps our resources allocated to our priorities.

Second, along this same line of thinking, focusing on our real needs improves our money-management skills. No longer will unrealistic wants influence our purchasing decisions. No longer will we be influenced by impulse-buying habits. By focusing our financial resources on our needs, we are able to set a realistic budget and stick to it. We're able to save for a rainy day and not be caught off guard by unexpected expenses. Most importantly, focusing on real needs allows us to manage our money more wisely and live within our means.

Third, just as focusing our financial resources on our real needs improves our money-management skills, focusing on our real needs also frees up more time to spend with those we really care about. Unrealistic wants have a tendency, as it controls our money, to control our time. As one desire is satisfied, another one is created. As a result, we can never be satisfied for long. Over time, we lose sight of what is really important when we start using our resources searching for things that never bring us lasting satisfaction. When this happens, we no longer control our time; unrealistic wants control it. Focusing our time on our real needs allows us to find time for the important people and activities in our lives.

Fourth, focusing on our real needs brings happiness to our lives. The influence of unrealistic wants convinces us that we need something better than what we have. When we chase unrealistic wants, we waste our resources looking for a greener pasture and quit enjoying the pasture we live in. Focusing our resources on our real needs allows us to be happy wherever we are and along the path to our destination.

Finally, focusing on our real needs allows us to develop patience. A good portion of our lives is spent waiting. We wait on an important telephone call. We wait in line at the store. We wait on the right job to come along. We wait on a suitable partner to marry. We are constantly waiting on someone or something. Keeping our attention focused on our real needs allows us to stop worrying about the future and permits us to live in the present. It allows us to focus on the now and not worry about what may be around the next corner. Focusing on our real needs increases our patience and allows us to enjoy life as it should be, in the moment.

Focusing on our real needs not only makes our lives better, it also makes the world a better place to live. Consider this for a moment: what if everyone in the world lived their lives focused on their real needs? Think about the difference it would make in all our lives. For example, hunger in the world would be eradicated. Children would not go to bed hungry because people around the world would not hoard their food, only use what they need, and share the remainder with the less fortunate.

Our cost of living would go down because there would be no reason for companies to charge exorbitant prices. They would only charge and make profits based on their real needs.

Disease would be reduced or wiped out in the world. Finding cures and developing medicines to treat the sick would not depend on the market viability of a product before it was manufactured and administered.

Financial crises in the world would be eliminated. Everyone—including countries—would live within their means and not overextend their financial resources.

The family unit would be strengthened. People would have more time to spend with their loved ones and on the important things in their lives.

Suffice it to say the world would be a better place if everyone lived their lives focused on their real needs. When you think about it, unrealistic wants affect our lives every day and in every corner of the world, more than you or I could ever imagine.

During my junior year of college, I took a job with a large paper manufacturing company in Florence, Alabama. At the time, this company had thirty-two plants in their Corrugated Box Division. My plant was a part of this division. We made every kind of shipping container possible.

For the next two years until I graduated from college, I worked on several different jobs throughout the plant. I was a general laborer, first helper, and machine operator on several machines. Upon graduation, the company offered me a management position, and I became the supervisor responsible for the most expensive machine in our plant. As a result of this promotion, I began supervising the crew I was a member of just the day before.

A couple of years later, the corporate office announced it was going to close the Florence, Alabama, plant. The plant was fairly old and wasn't as profitable as the company wanted it to be. I guess management determined that it would cost too much to modernize the plant and bring it up to today's standards, so they decided to shut it down. In the process, the company lost a lot of good people. I was lucky. I was one of only five people at my plant offered an opportunity to transfer to another shipping-container plant within the company.

When the call for the opportunity came in, I was in Memphis, Tennessee, in the waiting room at Baptist Hospital. Just hours before, my father, had a benign tumor removed from his pituitary gland. The general manager of the plant called me to see if I would come for an interview in Franklin, Kentucky, on Thursday of that week. My father was recovering well, and I needed a job, so I agreed to leave Memphis and my wife, and I drove back to Florence, Alabama, the next morning. The following day I drove to Franklin, Kentucky.

The interview and discussions went well, and I accepted a production scheduler's job and reported to work on the following Monday morning. Let me recap, I received the call for the job opportunity on Tuesday in Memphis, Tennessee, drove back to Florence, Alabama, on Wednesday, interviewed on Thursday in Franklin, Kentucky, accepted the job on Saturday, and started work on Monday in Franklin. In only six days, I totally transformed my life and transplanted my wife and myself 190 miles away from both our hometown and our families.

For the next six weeks, I lived out of a hotel in Bowling Green, Kentucky, and commuted about seventeen miles to work each day. My wife stayed in Alabama to complete her teaching contract at a local school. The day after the school year ended, she and our belongings moved to Franklin, Kentucky.

The two years that followed my arrival at the Franklin plant were hectic. Our plant acquired several new accounts, and we were breaking all previous sales and profit records. It was a tremendous growth period for our plant that kept us all busy. Life seemed good.

In October of 1983, just months after our son Jonathan was born, my company's only bag plant began contract negotiations with its local union. The plant was located in Pine Bluff, Arkansas—a town about forty-two miles southeast of Little Rock. The plant made every kind of paper bag you can imagine. If your product shipped in a bag—dog food, fertilizer, cement, or whatever—it made it.

The strike deadline was getting close, and the other corrugated container plants, including ours, went on alert. The plan was to send management personnel from each of the other thirty-two corrugated shipping container plants in to run the bag plant if the union went on strike. We would not be there to take their jobs, but to keep the plant running until their contract differences could be resolved. At the time, the bag industry was very competitive, and we didn't have another bag plant to shift the work to if there was a strike. As it was explained to us, we would be there only to run the plant and help the company keep its customer base to avoid layoffs once the strike was settled. Of course, the local union didn't see it that way.

Within a few days of the alert, contract negations completely broke down. A strike was inevitable, and the emergency plan was executed. I was offered a 15 percent increase in my current salary with all expenses paid if I agreed to go to Pine Bluff, Arkansas, to help run the plant. At the time, it seemed like a great opportunity to make a little extra money. Our first child had been born just a few months earlier, and money was tight. I had no idea how expensive diapers and baby formula were until after our son was born.

Within forty-eight hours of the plan execution, about thirty of us from other corrugated plants around the country converged on Arkansas to help run the plant and maintain its customer base. I flew into Little Rock, Arkansas, and was met at the airport by Mrs. Thompson, the plant manager's secretary. As we stood in the baggage claim area waiting for my bag, we made small talk about the plant and the community around it. She thanked me for coming and hoped my stay would be short and pleasant.

All I could think about was leaving my wife and child behind and wondering how they would get along without me. I left my family behind to pursue an opportunity that I hoped would be in the best interest of all of us. The fear of uncertainty controlled my thoughts as I waited for my luggage to arrive.

Several minutes had passed since we arrived in the baggage claim area, and all the other passengers on my plane had claimed their luggage and left. The conveyer belt stopped, and my bag was nowhere to be found. Everything I brought with me was in that bag, and I didn't have a clue where it was. As I found out later, neither did the airline. They promised to find my bag and bring it to me when it arrived. It arrived at the hotel two days later.

From the airport, Mrs. Thompson and I drove the remaining thirty or forty minutes to Pine Bluff. Little was said during this time. I spent most of the drive staring out the window, thinking about my family and my lost bag. I think Mrs. Thompson was sorry that my trip had started out this way and didn't quite know what to say.

When we arrived at the front gate of the plant, I was terrified at what I saw. There were angry people everywhere. It's not that I didn't expect to see a few people walking a picket line, but I was overwhelmed by the size of the crowd. There must have been a hundred people milling around carrying derogatory signs about the company and its management team. As they stood in front of the car, blocking the entrance, I was scared and truly feared for my life. Their faces showed pain and anger as we moved forward literally an inch at a time, parting the crowd as they yelled at us. As the last person moved to the side, we quickly drove through the gate and up the drive to the plant entrance.

After we parked, we quickly went inside where I met the general manger of the plant. He briefed me on the situation and told me where I could help. Just before we left his office he asked me for any item—clothes or identification—that had the company name or logo on it. Because of the threats the union had made, it would not be safe for me to carry these items while in Pine Bluff. Anything that identified me to the local union members and connected me to the company could get me hurt. No one told me about this before I left my plant, and quite frankly, with the thought of my family in the forefront of my mind, I was ready to go home.

For the next few months, we worked seven days a week, fourteen to sixteen hours a day. There were only enough of us to work skeleton crews on the machines, and, to make up for lost productivity, we worked long hours. Our days ran together after about a month, and most of the time I was there, I didn't even know the day of the week.

Armed guards with shotguns guarded not only the entrances to the plant, but also walked throughout the interior of the building as we worked, protecting us from the potential danger just outside the plant walls. Lunch and dinner was brought in or prepared at the plant each day to keep us from having to cross the picket line any more often than necessary. At the end of the workday, we piled into a caravan of station wagons and left together; each station wagon, one in front of the other, stayed within inches of each other as we slowly made our way through the crowd, parting the sea of people waiting for us at the gate. Understandably, we fought for the center seats of each vehicle, thinking that it would provide us the most protection from a gunshot in case someone in the crowd pulled a weapon. The next day at five o'clock in the morning, the process began again as we made our way back into the plant.

We spent our nights in our hotel rooms, not venturing out of our rooms or off the hotel property very often for fear of what may happen if union workers confronted us. From time to time, we changed hotel locations, trying to stay as safe as possible. We worked, we ate, and we slept. This was our entire existence.

Every night I called home to check on my family back in Franklin, Kentucky. I looked forward to this time each day, and, to be honest, the sound of my wife's voice kept me going. She described her day in detail and gave me mental images of our home to review in my head during the next day.

Our conversation each night centered on our son, Jonathan. He was growing and maturing, and I couldn't wait to find out what he had done each day. I hated to be away, but at the time, the influence of unrealistic wants convinced me that it was the right thing to do. The strike could be settled any day, according to the negotiators, and it was just a matter of time before we would be sent home to our families.

The promise of a quick resolution and returning home changed for me about a month into our stay. While talking to my wife one night on the phone as she described her day, she mentioned that Jonathan sat up by himself for the first time. I know this may sound silly, but I was devastated. My heart sank in my stomach. All I could think about was that I missed my son's first time to sit up on his own.

My life changed at that moment. The priorities of my life came into perspective that night. *What am I doing in Pine Bluff, Arkansas?* I asked myself. *We don't need the money that badly. We could get by on what we made.* My unrealistic wants influenced my decision, confused my priorities, and made me miss a major milestone in my son's and family's life.

I wanted to fly home that night. I didn't want to be in Pine Bluff, Arkansas, any longer. I didn't care how much money I could potentially make; I wanted to go home—now. I wanted to be with my wife and son where I belonged.

I didn't sleep at all that night, and it was all I thought about as I arrived at the plant early the next morning. As I walked into the building, I approached the plant manager and requested to return home. I will never forget the conversation that followed. It was clear that he had no concern for my family or me. His only concern was his plant. In the end, he refused to allow me to return home. In his opinion, the negotiations were nearing completion, and he felt that if I returned home at this critical time, others would soon follow. He went as far as stating that if I left without permission, he would call my plant manager ahead of my arrival, and he assured me that I would not have a job when I got there.

The next few weeks were very difficult. Christmas was approaching, and the hopes of returning home before the holidays decreased a little each day. The thoughts of not returning home were almost unbearable. These were some of the most difficult days of my life. I promised myself in Pine Bluff, Arkansas, that I would never allow anyone or anything to separate me from my family again.

A few days before Christmas, to everyone's surprise, the strike was resolved, and we were allowed to go home. We were all on planes returning home within hours of the papers being signed. Although we felt good about what we had accomplished, the union never really accepted our purpose for being there. As a result of our efforts, we retained most of the company's customers, protected the local jobs, and kept our company's bag plant profitable. More importantly for me, because of my unrealistic wants and the unrealistic wants of all of those involved in this event, I learned a lot about myself. My time in Pine Bluff, Arkansas, allowed me to reevaluate my life and understand what was really important to me.

When I arrived home, I took a few days off and spent it with my family enjoying the Christmas holidays. It was good to be with my wife and son again and take pleasure in their company. It was good to be home and to feel safe again. It was good to be removed from the stresses and the tensions of the past few months. The time off allowed me to reflect further on the priorities of my life and make some concrete decisions about how I lived it.

Through this experience, I learned how the influence of unrealistic wants affected my life. Because of the promise of a little extra money, I allowed myself to be taken away from my young family. I left the safety of my family dangerously uninformed about the situation ahead of me and was placed in a highly unstable environment that risked not only my life, but the future of my family. Most important, I allowed the lure of money to cause me to miss an important milestone in my son's life, a moment in time I will never get back.

Unrealistic wants are a powerful influence. Left unchecked, they can change your life in ways you cannot imagine. Don't let the influence of unrealistic wants confuse the priorities in your life as I let it confuse mine. Don't let unrealistic wants influence or direct your life in any way. Only you can eliminate the influence that unrealistic wants has on you. Only you can remove the influence unrealistic wants has on your decisions.

Are you living your life focused on your real needs? If not, why not? Focusing on your real needs will change your life. It will increase your satisfaction, make your life simpler, and allow you to find true happiness based on the priorities in your life.

How do we determine our real needs and distinguish them from unrealistic wants? Real needs are the basis of a simple life. Defining and knowing our real needs is important, but equally important is using them as our driving force to keep our lifestyle focused on what is important, our priorities. As we make decisions about how we use our resources, our real needs keep us on track, making decisions in line with our life goals.

Let's define what a need is. According to the *Encarta Dictionary*, a need is "something that is required, necessary, or essential." Think about it this way: a need is something we cannot live without and is essential to our happiness.

Although people categorize needs in different ways, I look at needs from two perspectives. The first type I define as basic needs or first-level needs. These needs are essential to life itself. Without them, life would not exist. For example, needs in this category would include food, water, or any other basic need that maintains life.

Beyond our most basic needs are second-level needs that provide comfort to our lives. These needs are established through the likes and dislikes of each individual. Some are created as the result of a personal experience while others are established through the direct or indirect influence of others. Either way, these needs are created because of personal decisions. Things in this category would include everything above the first level needs such as a cable TV subscription, a gym membership, or season tickets to your favorite football team.

Here is where the lines get a little blurry. Because second-level needs are so personal in nature, what one person considers an essential need, another person may consider unreasonable or unnecessary. For example, a few years ago I had a friend who said that his wife drives only a Volvo. In his opinion, there was no other car that compared to the Volvo, and he wouldn't let his wife drive anything less. In his mind, the Volvo, because of his perceived value of the car—right or wrong—made the car a real need and absolute bare minimum necessity.

On the other side of this argument, some people may perceive a car like the Volvo as an unnecessary expense. In their minds, a 1972 Honda

Civic is perfectly acceptable. It is a reliable car that gets good gas mileage and, most important, gets them from point A to point B. In their minds, their second-level need for transportation specifies only basic, dependable transportation. Whether our second-level need for transportation specifies a Volvo or a 1972 Honda, we can see that each could be considered an essential need to different people.

Our goal here is not to always pick the least expensive option to fulfill our need for something. Our goal is to determine the right level of need we must maintain to be satisfied. When I say what is your "real need," this is what I am talking about. The question you must ask yourself is what is my baseline need requirement to be happy?

Just as each person may define his or her real needs differently, every need has a different resource requirement. Obviously, if our baseline or real need to be happy is a Volvo, the resources required to support this need are greater than for a 1972 Honda. If our store of resources will support a Volvo, and it allows us to meet the other resource requirements of all our priorities, and if it's right for us and is the true baseline of our happiness, a Volvo is an acceptable real need. However, if we would be just as happy with a 1972 Honda, we need to reconsider the use of our resources. We should never use more resources than are necessary to meet our baseline happiness requirement. In fact, if we would be just as happy with a 1972 Honda, we are wasting our limited resources on something that could be used to support a more important priority.

Not only is it important to understand what a real need is or what it could be, it is just as important to understand what it's not. More than just something that is not required, necessary, or essential; a need that is considered more than a real need is gratuitous, unjustified, and unwarranted. At this point, it becomes an unrealistic want instead of a real need. Our resources are limited, and because of this, we should always make sure that our resources are being used to support our priorities, not unrealistic wants. When we waste our resources on unnecessary needs because of unrealistic wants, we lose focus on our priorities. When we lose focus on our priorities, we lose control of our lives.

Next, we will continue to expand on this topic and begin discussions about how to live a needs-based lifestyle. After all, our ultimate goal is to live a simpler life. Focusing on our real needs and priorities is the first step toward reaching our goal.

Living a Needs-Based Life

The first step in living a simple life is living a lifestyle based on our real needs and eliminating unrealistic wants. Now, I know what you are thinking. If unrealistic wants are such a major part of our society and they have been influencing our lives since the beginning of time, how can we just turn them off? How can we walk away from an influence that has controlled our world for centuries? Believe it or not, we have already taken the first step. Just understanding how unrealistic wants have influenced history and acknowledging that they continue to be a part of our daily living is the first step toward living a simple life.

Now that we understand how unrealistic wants influence the world and our lives, they can control us only if we allow them to. We have the power to control them. We have the power to turn off their influence in our lives. When we do this, we take the first step toward controlling our destiny.

Now, I am not naive enough to think that turning off this influence is as simple as turning off a light. This kind of thinking is completely embedded into the fabric of our society. It influences our thoughts and our behavior and can even cloud our understanding of what is right or wrong. Most people don't even consider how unrealistic wants affect their lives and the choices they make. However, once we take control of our thoughts and start living our lives based on our real needs, our lives become simpler, happier, and easier to manage.

It's no secret. None of us should be surprised that eliminating the influence of unrealistic wants from our lives takes commitment. Does a world-class athlete become world-class by taking a casual approach to his or her sport? Of course not, world-class athletes live their sport 24-7. They know that to be successful and to be considered among the elite takes dedication, hard work, and a commitment to be the best.

Just like world-class athletes and the commitment they make to their sport, we must make the same commitment to erase the influence that unrealistic wants has on our lives. We must fight the pressures that unrealistic wants put on our limited resources and be diligent not to let them control who we are or let them manipulate the decisions we make. If we can do this, we will enrich our lives beyond belief and open our eyes to possibilities we have only dreamed about.

So how do we turn off the persuasive influence unrealistic wants have on our lives and our decisions? We must develop a strong core-value system that will give us a measurable standard to evaluate the messages that bombard us every day so we can determine their real value and application to our lives. Likewise, we must use this same system to keep us focused on our priorities and moving down the life-path we have chosen. Developing a strong core-value system and committing to these values is essential to turning off the influence that unrealistic wants has on our lives.

Step One: Establishing a Strong Core-Value System

What are the core values we must develop to keep us focused on our priorities? First, before we can do that, we must understand what a value is and how it relates to a core value. A value is a belief that defines who we are as a person. A value is a consistent guiding force that defines how we evaluate and think and how we react to people and events in our lives. Like a value, a core value is the basis of our belief structure that all other beliefs or values are built upon. As in math, a core value is the least common denominator of our value system on which our entire belief system is built.

Our values come from many places. Our parents develop some of our values by repeatedly saying things like "Eat all of the food on your plate."

"Cover your mouth when you chew." "Respect your elders." "Take your hat off when you come into the house." "Wash your hands after you use the restroom." Over time, these messages or value statements become embedded within our belief structure and become part of our overall value system.

My mother, like all mothers everywhere, had hundreds of values she imparted to her children. She never let an opportunity go by to teach us something she felt was important to our development. Perhaps the most memorable value she imparted to us was "never leave the house wearing dirty underwear." Now, I know what you are thinking. How can wearing clean underwear be considered a value that one should live by? For me to answer this question, you must understand my mother. To my mother, being clean and presentable was important. She was afraid that one of us would get injured while we were away from our home. She wanted to make sure that if we had to go to the hospital and it was necessary to remove our clothing to treat our injury, our underwear was clean and presentable. To her, as silly as it may seem to some of you, clean underwear was a direct reflection on her ability to parent. Did her belief or value have an effect on me? Sure it did. Not only did I try to pass this value on to my own children every teachable moment I had, until this day, I never leave my home without wearing clean underwear. My underwear may be old and have holes in them, but they are always clean.

Just as we pick up values from our parents, we also collect values from people outside our family unit. The first one that comes to my mind came from American union workers: "Buy American." Even in a global economy where it is sometimes hard to determine where a product is manufactured, it is a value that many people still live by today. All things being equal, I "Buy American" because it keeps American workers employed.

Many of our values come from religious teachings. "Love one another" is a good example. However, as many people have discovered, living by this value is not easy. Because of all the intolerance and bigotry in the world, at times, loving everyone seems almost impossible. Although not easy to find, some people live their lives by this value.

"Don't judge others" is another value gained through religion. The Bible instructs us to remove the plank from our eye before we ask someone to remove the speck from their eye. Here, again, this value teaches us to focus on our own faults and discourages us from looking for faults in others.

Just as there are positive values and beliefs that we live our lives by, there are negative values that sometimes get in the way and taint who we are. We allow beliefs that are detrimental to us to infiltrate our value system and stain our character. It can happen through inappropriate associations, ignorance, and misplaced intentions. It most often happens because of a weak or underdeveloped core-value system.

As I mentioned before, I worked for a large paper-manufacturing company early in my career. This company ran a management training school just outside of Columbus, Ohio, in a little town called Mt. Vernon. The school ran one week a month for six months. I was lucky enough to be one of a few people from the Florence, Alabama, plant selected to attend the school with other supervisors from other plants around the country.

For six intense weeks, leaders in our company and experts in the industry inundated us with everything about our business. Although I had worked in the Florence plant for over two years, I had no idea how involved or complicated our business was or what it took to be successful in our industry. By the end of the training, we were exposed to everything about the operation of our plant and working in our industry.

When I was first asked to attend the school, I was a little apprehensive. I was young and hadn't done a lot of traveling. In addition, I would be attending class with people much older than I and more experienced in the workings of a shipping-container plant.

On our first trip to Columbus, Ohio, we were met by the director of the school in the Columbus airport. He had our flight numbers and communicated to us that he would be holding a sign in the waiting area of the gate identifying himself. Of course, I am dating myself here. This was obviously before September 11, 2001, when people were allowed to go to the gate and wait for arriving passengers. Okay, it was 1980. I was twenty-two. I was young, apprehensive, and uncertain about what I was getting into.

The director was waiting with the sign when I got off the plane, just as he promised. There were several other students waiting with him when I introduced myself. He suggested that we go down to the airport lounge, get acquainted, and wait while he collected a few others who had not yet arrived.

The next several minutes were entertaining to say the least. As we sat in the lounge waiting for others to arrive, we went around the table introducing ourselves by telling which plant we represented and adding any other small talk related to our job or responsibilities back at our plant. Sitting directly across from me at the table was a gentleman from upstate New York. Immediately, I noticed a keen interest in his voice in me. He seemed to focus his attention on me from the moment we sat down.

After a few minutes, he confirmed my suspicion and directed a question to me. "Do people in Alabama wear shoes?" he asked in a solemn voice. As I pondered his question, my mind ran rampant with thoughts. *Was he serious? Was he just trying to be funny? Is he crazy? How do I answer him?* Before I could even compose a response, he further clarified his question. "I have always been told that people in Alabama do not wear shoes. Is this true?" he asked.

Somewhere along his life journey, someone suggested to him that people in Alabama didn't wear shoes. From the tone in his voice, I was sure his question was sincere, and he truly believed that Alabamians did not wear shoes.

My first reaction was one of disgust. How could anyone in the twentieth century believe that people in Alabama didn't wear shoes? Was he slamming the people of my state? Was he implying that Alabamians are too poor to afford shoes? Was he making a personal attack on me? He had known me for less than thirty minutes. How could he ask such a question?

Before I responded, I collected myself and decided to play it off. I reached down, pulled off a shoe, and sat it on the table in front of him. Without hesitation, I expressed in as serious a voice as I could muster, "These are the first shoes I have ever owned." Without a smile I went on to tell him, "I bought them so I could come to the class. I had to go all the way to the Georgia state line to purchase these shoes, and they are hurting my feet. Would you mind if I took them off?" I asked. The table fell uncomfortably silent. I can only imagine what was going through the minds of the other people sitting there that day before I broke the tension with a laugh.

They say you only get one chance to make a good first impression. Because of his genuine belief that people in Alabama didn't wear shoes, he made an impression on me that remains with me even today. For the next six weeks, I made a concerted effort to dispel his many beliefs about the people of Alabama. By the end of the class, I considered us good friends.

My point is that we gather our value system from many different sources. We develop it through our family, friends, religious influences, and sometimes even complete strangers. As we hear and experience these value messages, we must be careful to filter the meaning of these messages against our core values. We must make sure the values we accept and hold dear are consistent with our basic beliefs and reflect the person we want to be and present to the world.

Some values or beliefs are positive, whereas others are not so positive. We must be careful to choose the values we live by and not let values or beliefs that are not in agreement with who we are get in the way of our decision making. If a value or belief doesn't measure up to our core values, we must eliminate it from our belief system. We must make certain that an incompatible value never catches the light of day and takes root in our belief system. Otherwise, our core values will be in a constantly confused state, and we will send mixed messages about who we are to others. More important, it will be virtually impossible for us to evaluate the messages of others and define who we are or how we should live our lives.

How do we evaluate the values we hold dear? We do so by developing strong core values that we measure all other values and beliefs against. Our core values are the basis of our entire belief system. To say it another way, our core values are the first row of blocks in our foundation that all other blocks or values are laid upon. To make our foundation strong enough to build our home, the first row of blocks must be durable to support the weight of the other blocks. Otherwise, over time, the foundation will collapse, and the home we have built will fail.

You may have others, but for this discussion, there are five core values that are vitally important to measuring all other values and beliefs against and to eliminating the influence unrealistic wants has on our lives: always do what is right, tell the truth when it counts, accept responsibility for our actions, treat others as we want to be treated, and live within our means. These five core values are the basis of a needs-focused belief system. Working together, they form a strong core-value system that allows us to evaluate our options, eliminate unrealistic wants, and live life more simply. Let's look at each one individually.

Core Value One: Always Do What Is Right

Always doing what is right, while it may negatively affect us from time to time, is the basis of any core-value system. Doing the right thing in any situation is vital to living a simple life.

Always doing the right thing benefits us in four ways. First, it makes our lives easier. We don't have to be concerned about or lose sleep over the decisions we make. When we don't need to worry about the decisions we make, our lives naturally become less complicated. Our stress level decreases because we know in our hearts we did the right thing.

Second, always doing what is right decreases our concern about the consequences of our actions when something goes wrong. What is the first thing people do when something goes wrong? We look for someone to blame. When we always do the right thing, we can keep a clear conscience knowing that based on the information we had at the time of the decision, we did everything possible to do the right thing.

Third, not only does doing the right thing make our lives easier and decrease our concerns when something goes wrong, it simplifies and streamlines our decision-making process. By not allowing this core value to waver, we can make decisions much more quickly and feel confident that our decisions are true to who we are. No longer do we need to mull over other options that might be bouncing around in our heads. When we know up front that we are going to do the right thing no matter what, there is no reason to consider anything else.

Finally, and perhaps most important, always doing the right thing allows us not only to control our unrealistic wants more effectively, but when used in conjunction with our other core values that we will discuss later, it allows us to live our lives more simply. Think about it. When we commit ourselves to always doing the right thing, many of the unrealistic wants or temptations we encounter go away. We are not tempted to buy something we don't need, spend time on things that bring no value to our lives, or participate in something that is not a priority. When we erase temptations because it is the right thing to do, we simplify our lives.

In 1996, I left a secure job with the City of Louisville, Kentucky, to join a startup company. The new company promoted themselves as a secure underground storage facility for archival records of all types. The parent company is heavily involved in mining limestone quarries and felt underground storage could be a natural extension of its business. After a nationwide search, the company selected me as the VP of Operations. It was a good move for my career and my family.

At the time of my joining the new startup, construction of the underground facility was well on its way. It was a massive 570,000 square feet facility, 60 feet underground in northern Kentucky. Millions of dollars had already been spent, and construction was scheduled to be completed within six to eight months. It was impressive by any standard.

Being highly experienced in the records and information management field, my role in the beginning was to evaluate the business plan and contact potential customers until construction could be completed. Once open for business, my role would be to oversee the operations of the facility.

Within a few weeks of joining the company, I discovered several errors in its business plan and in the layout of the facility. In addition, through contacts with potential customers, I learned that most of the interest in our facility was not to store archival records, but to locate a data center within the confines of the underground facility. The errors in the business plan were not showstoppers in my opinion, but they would bring to light questions about the company's projected revenue.

At my first opportunity, I discussed the findings with my boss. A few days later, he and I met with senior members of the parent company and shared my concerns. It was not a happy meeting, but I knew in my heart that it was the right thing to do. I couldn't just let the leaders go blindly down the path they were heading and not alert them to my findings. In preparation for the meeting, I prepared drawings and proposed ideas to correct the errors I had found.

Telling you that the meeting was not a happy meeting is an understatement. You could tell, through the executive team member's facial expressions and their sighing, this was not what they wanted to hear. I felt terrible for my boss and all those involved in the new startup, but I felt it was my duty to share the mistakes I had found. It was the right thing to do.

Management quickly assigned a financial guru to my sales projection worksheets, as any company would do, to go through the numbers I presented. For the next several months, we refined the numbers while construction of the facility continued. Although the new sales projections and business plan reduced the company's return on investment and made the new venture not as appealing to the parent company as originally anticipated, I continued to contact potential customers. However, the main theme I continued to hear from potential customers was that they were more interested in data center space. The parent company didn't have any experience in operating a commercial data center and were not interested in increasing its capital requirements to venture into unknown territory.

The week before Christmas, I presented the final set of numbers to my boss, who was to meet with the CEO of the parent company a few days later. We massaged the numbers as best we could, and although the numbers were aggressive, we felt they were achievable and would provide a nice profit to the parent company.

I spent the rest of the holiday season with my family. I was afraid that the numbers would not be satisfactory to the owners, but telling them there was a problem with their business plan was the right thing to do. Although I was concerned about the outcome of the meeting, I felt no remorse about my actions and enjoyed a wonderful holiday season with my family.

The week after New Year's, my boss and I met with the senior management team of the parent company. Before the meeting started, a senior vice president of the parent company leaned across the table and asked me if I could still go back to my former position with the city. At that moment, I knew a decision had been made about my future. The return on investment with the startup company was not sufficient for the parent company, and within a few days, my boss and I were terminated, and construction of the startup company was put on hold.

The termination of the startup company was a huge blow to all of us, but especially to my boss. He had worked for the parent company for decades, and the outcome of my findings resulted in his separation from the parent company and the startup company he had nurtured. Although I felt terrible about what had happened, I knew deep inside that I did the right thing when I made senior management aware of the issues facing the startup company. I was prepared for the consequences I faced because of my actions. At the same time, I hoped the parent company would be fair to my boss because of his decades of undying loyalty to them. A week later, I was given a fair separation package, and I no longer worked for the parent company.

But this is not the end of the story. In fact, although things looked bleak after the startup company was discontinued, the chain of events that brought us to this point turned out to be the best thing that ever happened to me. Although the next few months were difficult for my former boss, I think in retrospect he would also agree that everything worked out for the best.

Within a few months, the parent company rehired my former boss to restart the venture, not as a records and information storage facility, but as a commercial data center. After his termination, he continued to talk to the parent company and pitched the idea about the data center. They eventually agreed to start a new venture in the commercial data center industry. My former boss was rehired as the president of this new company, and he built a successful commercial data center that provided the return on investment the parent company required.

As for me, I received many benefits from the failed company startup. First, because of the physical examinations necessary for me to acquire key person insurance as a member of the executive team, I discovered I had elevated blood sugar levels, a discovery that perhaps will allow me to live a longer life now that I am getting the proper treatment. Second, the severance package I received upon separation from the company allowed me to start my own successful consulting business that, up until then, I never had the resources to start. Third, it allowed me to work from home and homeschool my son during some difficult times in his life. Finally, because I was working from home, I had more time to spend with my family, which was the greatest benefit of all.

Did I do the right thing when I told senior management about its business plan errors? Absolutely! Not only was it the right thing to do at the time, it ended up being a blessing in disguise for everyone involved. Although the situation looked bleak at the time the errors were brought out into the open, it worked out best for everyone involved: the parent company, my former boss, and me.

As this true story illustrates, we must be resolved always to do the right thing whatever the situation or however it may personally affect us.

How do we determine the right thing to do in all situations? First, we must get to the point in our lives where we not only trust the core-value system we've built within ourselves, we depend on it. We use it as our guiding light to keep us on track and focused. Second, we must honestly evaluate the issues and review our options. As best we can, we must try to understand the positive as well as the negative consequences of our actions to determine the best course of action. If we stay true to our core values, we reap all the benefits that come from them.

Will the values or beliefs we base our decisions on always be correct? No, sometimes regardless of how hard we try to drive these erroneous values out of our belief system, a rogue belief will slip in that is not consistent with our core values. Using our five core values as our guide, we must evaluate these rogue beliefs and eliminate them whenever necessary.

Will the outcomes of our decisions always turn out positively for everyone involved? No, it is virtually impossible to make everyone happy. Occasionally, despite our best efforts, doing the right thing will not have a positive outcome. However, the goal here is that, when considering all sides of the issues we face, we must always do what is right, even if it negatively affects us or those around us. Doing what is right is most important.

How do we determine what to do when we are faced with difficult decisions? We evaluate the issues, review our options, and attempt to understand the consequences of our actions. In the end, always try to do what is right. We must make doing the right thing a priority in our lives.

Always doing the right thing is important. It's important not only to keeping us on track with the decisions we make, but when used in conjunction with the other four core values, it forms a solid game plan to get us to the simple life.

Core Value Two: Tell the Truth

The second core value that helps us stay on track and live a simple life is telling the truth. No one ever said that telling the truth is easy, but it is the right thing to do. Telling the truth is only difficult when what we want people to know doesn't match up with what really happened. It's only human nature to want to make things seem better than they really are, but we must resist the temptation to skew the facts.

There are benefits to telling the truth. For one, it frees our conscience. We never have to worry that someone will dispute our account and embarrass us. If we tell the truth, there is nothing to worry about.

Just as it frees our conscience, telling the truth stops the perpetuation of other lies. No longer do we need to create additional lies to keep our story consistent with all the other lies we've told. Look at it this way: telling the truth allows us to always tell the truth. It clears our memory of never-ending lies and keeps us from having to craft others. When we tell the truth, the lies stop, and our lives get simpler.

Just as there are benefits to telling the truth, there can be negative consequences if our words are not weighed carefully. When I say "tell the truth," I'm not talking about telling the truth like in the movie *Invention of a Lie*. In this movie, everyone is brutally honest, and, because of it, every person is depressed and suicidal. In every scene, the actors are viciously honest down to the tiniest detail about one another's looks, mannerisms, and actions. As this movie clearly shows, no one wants to be reminded about how fat or ugly he or she is in every conversation, nor is this the kind of truth I am describing here. The truth I am describing is, when it counts and your words or actions matter, tell the truth.

My wife, Mary, and I have been married for thirty-four years. We met in the fourth grade when we sat across the aisle from each other in Ms. Shelton's class. It was not love at first sight. In fact, it wasn't until the eleventh grade that we started dating and looking seriously at each other with regards to the future. Not until our senior year of college, did we tie the knot. If you include the time we dated exclusively, we have been a couple for over forty years and acquaintances for over forty-six years. I can honestly say that she knows me better than anyone and is my best friend.

Now, don't get me wrong. We haven't been married for thirty-four years without a lot of hard work and the careful weighing of words. Being with someone for this length of time demands that you be able to bend in the wind like the grass in the field. You must be flexible and let things roll off your back from time to time.

As such, throughout our time together, there have been times when I have not always been as truthful with my wife as I could have been. There are times in any relationship when being brutally honest and truthful is not the best course of action. Occasionally, weighing our words carefully is necessary to keep the relationship on the right path. For example, when my wife asks me if she looks portly in a certain outfit, I don't answer by saying, "You look like Porky the Pig." No, I weigh my words carefully and try to determine what could be the consequences of the words I use. You see, I love her more than anything in the world, and I don't want to say or do anything that might be construed as something different. To be brutally honest, I don't care if she looks heavy in a particular outfit. If the outfit makes her happy, it makes me happy too! Her happiness and my relationship with her are more important to me than how she physically looks in a particular outfit.

This same reasoning is true in all parts of life. There are times when telling the truth will cause more harm than is necessary. There are going to be times when a little white lie doesn't hurt anybody, but allows us to resolve an issue gracefully. Sometimes more important issues are at stake than being brutally honest.

What I am trying to express when I say "tell the truth" is that when honesty means something in the important events of life, always tell the truth. When the outcome of our answer has measurable consequences, tell the truth.

The famous cliché "The truth will set you free" is accurate. If you always tell the truth, it sets you free from your conscience and you never having to cover your lies with other lies. Truth and honesty, when they matter, are not only important to living a needs-based lifestyle, they are essential to being happy and living a simple life.

One other important lesson should be learned about telling the truth: just as we should never lie to others in moments when it matters, we must never lie to ourselves. There will be times when our conscience will try to convince us that the real truth is something different from what we are expressing to others. There will be times when what we are saying is different from what we are feeling inside. We must pay attention to the little voice in our heads and our hearts and be honest with ourselves. If we can't be honest with ourselves, how will we ever be honest with others when it matters?

Telling the truth works hand in hand with always doing what is right. In fact, all the core values work together supporting each other to form a strong core-value system that allows us to live a needs-based lifestyle—the simple life.

Core Value Three: Accept Responsibility for Our Actions

We hear all the time how the new generation never accepts responsibility for its actions. The impression we get is that young people are quick to blame others for their mistakes. As far as I'm concerned, it is no different today than it was years ago. To our detriment, as a society we have always had trouble accepting responsibility for our actions.

Whatever the perception may be about the new generation, accepting responsibility for our actions is a key core value and is indispensable to living life more simply. Let's face it, there will be times when we mess up. And sometimes the consequences and ramifications of our actions when we mess up will be painful. Life happens, and there is nothing we can do to stop it. However, when we mess up, we must take responsibility for our actions and make it right.

I'm going to share something with you that I have told to every person who has ever worked for me. If you make a mistake, and it doesn't change the course of history or if no one will remember it in a hundred years, own up to your mistake and move on. Learn everything you can from your mistake, move on with your life, and try to avoid repeating the same mistake. I truly believe that if you are not making mistakes, you are not doing anything. In fact, more than likely you're stuck in a rut and are not working toward accomplishing anything.

If you have read anything I have ever written, you know that I believe it is inevitable that we will make mistakes. We're human and mistakes will happen. However, the more important point here is that we must accept responsibility for the mistakes we make. We must never try to shift the blame to someone else for an action we have taken. We must be honest with ourselves, do what is right, and take full responsibility for all our actions.

During the summer of my college sophomore year, I managed the city swimming pool in Muscle Shoals, Alabama. The original person hired to manage the pool left the area about three weeks into the season. At the time, I was working at the pool as a lifeguard. The park director thought I was the natural replacement, and he asked me to manage the pool for the remainder of the season. It was my first official management position.

About a month into the assignment—I'm going to date myself again here—the original *Star Wars* movie was released at the theater. My wife, Mary, and I were dating at the time, and we planned a night at the theater to see the new movie that was getting great reviews. Our friends spoke highly of the movie, and we couldn't wait to see it.

On the day of our planned date, the swimming pool was busy. Like anywhere, the more people you have packed into a limited space, the more issues you have with people getting along with each other. Tempers become aggravated when there is not enough space for people to spread out and stay out of one another's way. This day at the pool was no different. We had problems all day long.

Every day just before closing time, we went through a routine to prepare the pool for the next morning. As part of this practice, I backwashed the pool filter. For those of you not familiar with this process, to backwash the filter you reverse the flow of water from the pool and rinse all of the solid material like hair or leaves that have settled on top of the filter during the day down the drain. This process is necessary to keep the filter clean and working properly. At a public swimming pool, this procedure must be done daily.

While I backwashed the pool filter, I was paged to the office. It couldn't have been fifteen minutes before closing time when the page rang out over the PA system. When I arrived at the office, I found two young men being held apart by my lifeguards. A fight had broken out in the pool, and one of the boys had pulled a knife. Unbelievably, my smallest female lifeguard had jumped in the middle of them and broken up the fight. Because of her actions, no one was seriously hurt, but since a knife was involved, protocol required me to call the police.

Forty-five minutes after the incident occurred, the police took the boys off my hands, and I was free leave work. I rushed home, showered and changed clothes, and hurried to pick up my date to go see the *Star Wars* movie.

As we sat in the theater watching the beginning credits scroll across the screen, thoughts ran through my head about the incident that had just happened at the pool. *I can't believe my lifeguard jumped in the middle of two boys fighting,* I thought to myself. *One of the boys had a knife. She could have been hurt badly. I've told my lifeguards over and over to never jump in the middle of a fight, especially if someone has a weapon.* Then it hit me like a two-by-four, right between the eyes. *Did I turn off the backwash? Oh no! Did I turn off the backwash?* The thought of possibly leaving the backwash running water out of the pool down the drain sent panic throughout my entire body.

I quickly leaned over to Mary and told her I would be right back. I ran to the box office of the theater and asked if I could use their phone. While I dialed the number, I hoped the scuba diving class that was scheduled to meet that night had caught my mistake and reversed the water flow.

The phone rang and rang and rang. No one answered. I decided it would be necessary for me to drive over to the pool and check it out. The pool was only a few minutes away, and I needed to make sure everything was okay. If everything went well, I would be back shortly, and Mary would never know I left.

When I arrived at the pool, there was no one to be found. Unknown to me, the scuba diving class had been canceled. As I walked up to the gate to look inside, my heart sank into my stomach. No one had caught my mistake and the return pipes in the side of the pool were shooting water into the center of the pool like the water fountain in front of the Bellagio Hotel in Las Vegas, Nevada.

By the time I turned off the backwash, there were only eight inches of water in the shallow end of a pool that normally held four feet of water. For the past few hours, the backwash removed water from the pool and ran it down the drain into an empty lot adjacent to the pool. The once empty lot now looked like a small lake in the distance.

As soon as I had opened the faucets and started refilling the swimming pool with water, I went to see my boss, the director of the park. I remembered he was scheduled to attend a city meeting that night, and I hoped I could catch him before the meeting adjourned. I didn't want to tell him what had happened, but I knew I had to.

The five-minute drive to city hall was one of the longest drives I have ever made. All I could think about was losing my job. *How could I be so stupid and leave the backwash running?* I asked myself. I was sure this mistake would be the end of my first management position.

I had plenty of excuses I could have used. I could have blamed the incident on the fight at the end of the day. I could have blamed it on the police officers that kept me long after the pool closed. I could have blamed it on my other lifeguards and said they should have noticed the backwash was running before they left for the day. I could have said that if the scuba class had not canceled someone would have stopped the backwash. But I didn't use any of those excuses. It was my fault, and I was prepared to accept my fate for making this costly mistake.

As I looked at my boss through the small window in the door of the conference room, I motioned for him to come out into the hallway. My voice broke as I told him the news. I was devastated about what had happened, and I was expecting him to fire me on the spot.

As he paused to gather his thoughts, a big smile came across his face. He began to laugh out loud. "Water is shooting into the pool like a waterfall?" he laughingly asked. He told me to go back to the theater, and he would check on the pool after his meeting. He told me that he would see me bright and early at the pool the next morning. I was relieved! Although his action would have been justified, he didn't fire me.

Although I didn't lose my job that night for the mistake I made, there were consequences I had to endure as a result of my actions. Refilling the pool with water cost the city a lot of money. As best we could calculate the next morning, 150,000 gallons of water had drained out of the pool. As a result, we closed the pool to the public for two days and stopped all diving in the diving well for a few days after we reopened until it was safe again. For several days, we taught swimming lessons in the deep end of the swimming pool because there was not enough water in the shallow end.

However, the biggest consequence was the ridicule I received from my fellow workers the rest of the summer. At every opportunity, employees of the park ribbed me about the mistake I made. "Do you need to backwash the pool?" they would say. "I think the filter needs to be cleaned." Maintenance workers would shout comments out their truck windows to me as they drove past the pool. They made up cute little names for me like "backwash" to never let me forget what had happened. I was teased all summer long. But I didn't mind. Because I knew I deserved it. I was lucky to still have my job, and the consequences of my mistake were minor compared to what they could have been.

In retrospect, perhaps the largest consequence of the event personally was that I never got to see the movie *Star Wars*. By the time I got back to the theater and sat down in my chair, the ending credits were scrolling across the screen. It wasn't until 2008 while on vacation with my wife in the Great Smoky Mountains, some thirty-one years later, that I finally sat down to watch the movie with her. Our friends were right. It was a great movie.

I share this story only to illustrate the importance of always taking responsibility for your actions. Just like telling the truth when it counts, it's the right thing to do.

Why is taking responsibility for your actions important? Because taking responsibility makes you a man. If you are a female, it makes you a woman. This simple action sets us apart from our childhood ways and allows us to enter into adulthood.

As a child, we took every opportunity to shift the blame to someone else when we messed up. That's what children do. The perceived consequences of our actions, when we are children, far outweigh the benefits of owning up to our actions, and our fears prevent us from doing what is right. So we shift the blame.

As adults, we can no longer shift blame when we mess up. As adults, we know the difference between right and wrong. We know every action we take has a consequence. No longer can we hide behind our momma's coattail and blame our actions on someone else when something doesn't go as it should. That's not what adults do.

At this point, you may be asking yourself what does all this have to do with living the simple life? It's very simple. Accepting responsibility for our actions is an important core value. It works hand in hand with the other core values we have discussed about always doing the right thing and telling the truth. They all work together to build a sustainable value system that allows us to live a needs-based lifestyle. They complement each other and help us separate real needs from unnecessary wants. What happens when we focus our living on our real needs? Our lives get simpler.

Let's be honest. Any mistake or action we can take could be blamed on someone else if we thought about it long enough. However, we must fight the temptation to blame others for our missteps. Accepting responsibility for our actions is critical to being an adult, finding happiness, and living life more simply. By accepting responsibility for our actions, not only do we keep a worry-free conscience, we will be amazed at how others will respect us for being responsible. A real man—or woman—is one who accepts responsibility for his or her actions and endures the consequences that result from them.

Core Value Four: Treat Others as You Want to Be Treated

The Golden Rule is perhaps the most famous core value of all: treat others as you want them to treat you. By anyone's standard, these are wise words to live by.

If everyone lived by this one core value, the world would be a better place. With one value, we could eliminate all hate and war everywhere in the world. We could do away with mistrust and deception. We could eradicate theft and robbery. Honestly, if everyone made this core value an integral part of his or her life, we could eliminate almost every type of evil in the world.

Unfortunately, it will never happen. Why? Because we let our self-indulging nature get in the way. We allow it to convince us that we are better than others. We allow it to sway us into believing we deserve more privileges or rights than other people. It causes us to feel like we are more special than everyone around us, and we deserve to be treated differently. When this happens, our lives get complicated. Posturing ourselves for privileges or rights we may or may not deserve clouds our decision making and reduces our effectiveness.

How does it reduce our effectiveness? When we let our self-indulging nature get in the way, everything becomes a competition. Everything becomes a struggle as we compete with others trying to accumulate more privileges or rights than other people have. If we're not careful, over time our self-worth becomes our driving force. When this happens, our effectiveness in working with others diminishes. We must never forget that we all need people in our lives from time-to-time to help us be successful. We can't be successful if we allow our self-indulging nature to drive a wedge between us and the people we need in our lives the most.

Treating others as we want to be treated is a simple concept. There is nothing complicated about this idea. It doesn't take special education to understand. A little self-control could change the world if we would only apply this core value to our lives.

How do we want to be treated? How do we want people to interact with us? Do we want them to be respectful to us, or do we want them to be rude and impolite? How we treat others determines the environment for how we will be treated in return. If we show people disrespect, they will probably show disrespect for us. If we are cruel to people, they will probably be cruel to us. If we treat others as if we are better than them, shame on us. As my dad told me early in my life, "You are no better than anyone else. They put their pants on the same way you do—one leg at a time."

We all want people to respect us and listen to what we have to say. We all want people to see us as having value and to respect our opinions. We all want people to recognize us as equals and acknowledge that we matter. If we want people to respect us, we must first respect them. If we want people to value us, we must first value them. If we want people to treat us as equals, we must treat them the same way. We must model to others how we want to be treated.

So, what does this have to do with living the simple life? It has everything to do with it. If we allow our self-indulgence to control our thinking process, we will never rest. We will be in constant competition with everyone to make sure we get everything we think we deserve. Our focus will shift from a needs-based lifestyle to one controlled by unrealistic wants. Acting as if we are better than others, will reduce our opportunities for success because no one will want to be around us. Most important, self-indulgence will control our lives and cause us to lose focus on our priorities.

Don't let self-indulgence influence how you treat others! It will escort you down a path that will lead to the destruction of your character. How can you expect someone to treat you in a particular way if you don't first treat them in the manner you want to be treated? You are kidding yourself if you think otherwise. Treating everyone the way you want to be treated releases you from the temptation of self-indulgence, allows you to find happiness by simplifying your relationships, and permits you to live life more simply.

Core Value Five: Live within Your Means

A discussion about developing a strong core-value system and living a needs-based lifestyle would not be complete without talking about living within our means. This is also a simple concept that is easy to understand, but because of the controlling power of unrealistic wants, is seldom followed.

The United States is perhaps one of the best examples of this problem. We are a country with an out-of-control spending problem. As the debt in our country continues to grow exponentially, the financial future of the United States has come into question. As the current trend suggests, the debt growth is not sustainable. Although the implementation of the solution may be painful, the fix is simple. As a country, we must live within our financial means and stay focused on our priorities. We must not spend more than our financial resources will allow.

Just like our government, we sometimes live outside our financial means. Something catches our eye, and without considering the financial consequences or its ultimate effect on our life's priorities, we buy it. Living this way, if we're not careful, has the same consequences as it does for our country. We end up wasting our financial resources on things that have little or nothing to do with our life's priorities. When this happens, over time, we lose focus on what is really important, and our financial future becomes questionable.

How do we live within our financial means? Here again, it's simple: we never spend more than we can afford. We never put ourselves in a position that requires more resources than we have. We must turn away from bright, shiny objects and stay focused on our priorities to keep from purchasing something we do not need or cannot afford.

It starts with fully understanding the limits of our financial means. What is my net income after taxes? What are my expenses, both monthly and periodic? What is my net disposable income? How much can I spend on extras every month? I will go into more detail later, but for now, the question is, how much income must I maintain to meet my financial obligations? Not spending more than we have or can afford is a key core value.

In the early 1980's just after moving to Franklin, Kentucky, we purchased our second home. At the time, my wife and I were living in a duplex with one child and had another one on the way. Up until this point, we were reluctant to move to a larger place, but with the coming of our second child, we really didn't have a choice.

For the next several months, we looked for a suitable place to rent. We really didn't want to rent, but from the time I transferred with my company to Franklin, Kentucky, we thought it would be a short-term assignment, and we would be back in our home state of Alabama soon. Alabama is where our families were, and we hoped to be back there within a year.

Franklin, Kentucky, is a small town with a population, at the time, of about eight thousand people. It was a beautiful, little, two red-light town that was an ideal place to raise a family. However, small towns are notorious for lacking suitable housing, especially rental housing. We searched high and low and couldn't find anything to rent that would meet our needs.

Throughout our search, everyone told us we shouldn't rent, but should buy a house. "You're just throwing money down a rat hole," everyone told us. "You should purchase a house and get the tax benefits that come with owning it, and when you get ready to move back to Alabama, you can sell the house." We knew they were right, and when we couldn't find a place to rent, we contacted a real estate agent to help us search for a house to buy that would be suitable for our growing family. The way the housing market and the economy was growing it didn't seem like much of a risk at the time.

Within a few weeks, we found the perfect house. We knew it was the right place as soon as we drove up the driveway. During the next few days, we toured the house several times, asking all types of questions about the property. The owners were asking a little more than we thought we could afford, but the house was in a good location, and it had many of the amenities we were looking for.

We talked it over for a few days with our real estate agent, and we made an offer on the house. The price quickly became the sticking point as we offered and they counter offered. In the end, we came to an agreement. We probably still paid too much for the house, but the owners agreed to pay all closing costs. We were excited and couldn't wait to move in.

During the negotiation process, our real estate agent suggested we talk with a financial representative she worked with to secure a loan. We didn't really know anyone in town, and since her company worked with this financial company regularly, we agreed to meet with him.

A few days later, a gentleman came to our apartment to work out the details of a home loan. For hours we sat around our kitchen table going through the numbers. Just as we suspected, the house was a little out of our price range for a conventional loan, but we were told not to worry. He proceeded to tell us that his company had many other loan options that would fit our needs.

From this point forward, unrealistic wants controlled our thinking, and we made a series of mistakes. In hindsight, we should have walked away. We should have stopped the purchase process on this house and restarted our search with the new knowledge about how much we could really afford, but the influence of our unrealistic wants wouldn't allow it.

Over the next several hours, we discussed our options. In the end, we completed the paperwork for an adjustable rate mortgage with a balloon payment at the end of the thirty-year note. This loan provided us the monthly payment we could afford, and the payment couldn't adjust more than five percent every two years. He convinced us that with the strong economy and housing market we were in, even if the loan payment did adjust five percent every two years, with our yearly raises and the appreciation we were gaining on the house, we shouldn't have any trouble making the payment. Everything he said made perfect sense, and we went forward with the loan application.

A few weeks later, the loan was approved, and we set a closing date. A month later, we were moving into our new home. The house was perfect. It was just what we wanted. We loved this house and everything about it.

A few months later, as luck would have it, the economy went into a tailspin. The housing market began to weaken, inflation increased, and my employer's business started to decline. To keep from downsizing the company, the corporate office froze salaries across the entire company. It was a tough time for everyone.

The salary freeze remained in place for over two years. With the added expense of the new child, consumer prices rising, and my salary frozen, money was tight. Our adjustable rate mortgage was due to adjust, and, just as expected, our payment went up five percent. The promise of higher wages and a strong economy—the premise of our home purchase—was gone. Although we could meet our financial obligations, we meticulously had to watch how we spent our money.

A short time later, with a new job prospect, we moved to Louisville, Kentucky, about 130 miles north up Interstate 65. Our intentions of moving back to Alabama were put on hold once again, but never forgotten as we set out in a new direction. We hated to leave Franklin and our friends, but Mary and I felt it was the right thing to do.

The next year was the most difficult year of our lives. Even though I had a good job in Louisville and my wife was able to find a teaching job a short time later, the mistakes we made several years ago when we signed the loan documents at our kitchen table continued to haunt us. The economy was still in bad shape, the housing market continued to be depressed, and we couldn't sell our house in Franklin at the price we needed to cover the balance of our loan. We were upside down in our loan, and because of the type of loan we were locked into, we owed more on our house than we could sell it for.

Let me set the stage for you. We were living in Louisville, Kentucky, in an apartment. We had a home in Franklin, Kentucky, that we owed more on than we could sell it for. We had two decent jobs that should have been able to meet our financial obligations under normal circumstances, but because of the two monthly housing payments and the fact that the cost of living in Louisville was much higher than we anticipated, we were in financial trouble. In short, things were not going well. We were not meeting our financial obligations, and we were, as some would say, "robbing Peter to pay Paul."

Saying we weren't meeting our financial obligations is an understatement. We had creditors constantly calling us for their money. We were even borrowing money against our credit cards to pay bills. We were so broke and in debt that we couldn't even afford to fix the water pump on my car. Because it was leaking water so profusely, we had to carry milk jugs of water in the trunk of my car and stop every couple of miles to add water to my radiator to get from one place to the next. We were down and out and about to lose everything.

Just when we were about to turn off the lights and file bankruptcy, things started to turn around. We found a buyer for our home in Franklin, and although we took a five thousand dollar loss on the sale, we were eventually able to get out of our terrible loan commitment. In addition, my wife and I secured better jobs and increased our financial resources. Finally, we started seeing the light at the end of the tunnel. One costly mistake, sitting at our kitchen table, influenced by our unrealistic wants, almost changed our lives and, more importantly, the lives of our children for the foreseeable future.

The influence of unrealistic wants is powerful. It will ruin our lives if we let it control our thinking and decision making. My wife and I were lucky. We were able to wiggle out of its grip just before it changed our lives forever. Living and staying within our financial means is important to every part of our lives and essential to living a simple life.

However, living within our financial means is only one aspect of living within our total resources. Another part of living within our means is equally important: living within our time means.

Just as financial means relates to how we spend our money, time means relates to how we budget and spend our time. We all have twenty-four hours a day, 168 hours a week, to accomplish all the things that we need and want to achieve. How we spend our time directly affects our ability to live within our means and meet our obligations. Time is the most important resource in the world. No resource is more valuable.

Why is time so valuable? How we manage our time directly affects everything in our lives. It affects our family life. It affects our financial position. It affects our health. It affects our relationships with others. It affects our success. It affects our happiness. Literally, time affects everything in our lives. Just like our financial means, living within our time means allows us to focus our time on the more important things in our lives—our priorities.

Staying focused on our priorities and living within our means go hand in hand. Here's how: using our financial and time resources to support our priorities keeps us focused on the important things in our lives. In the big picture view, when we focus our money and time on our priorities, we simplify our lives. We should never use our limited resources on things that are not a priority. To ensure this doesn't happen, we must budget our money and time wisely and not allow distractions—unrealistic wants—to cause us to stray from the significant things in our lives. Staying within our means—money-wise and time-wise – frees up resources we can use to support our life's priorities.

For the last several pages, we have discussed the five values that make up our core-value system. They are do the right thing, tell the truth when it counts, accept responsibility for our actions, treat others as we want to be treated, and live within our means. These core values are meant to work hand in hand with each other to help us focus on a needs-based lifestyle—the simple life.

More important than just keeping us focused on a needs-based lifestyle, the five core values are the basis of who we are as people. They are the guiding force that defines how we evaluate, think about, and react to people and events in our lives. They are the basis of our belief structure on which all other beliefs or values are built. Working together, they form a strong core belief system that allows us to turn off the influence of unnecessary wants, simplify our lives, and find happiness.

Let's briefly look at each one again and pull them together into a cohesive unit to see how they work together, complementing each other to form a strong core-value system. First, doing what is right in any situation allows us never to worry about the decisions we make or the consequences of our actions. In any situation, we are resolved to do the right thing, even if it negatively affects us. We are able to make decisions more quickly and feel confident that the results of our decisions or actions are true to who we are. Doing the right thing helps us maintain a clear conscience and live guilt free.

Second, telling the truth when it matters demonstrates the level and depth of our character to others. People respect people who tell the truth when honesty has measurable consequences, particularly when the truth negatively affects us. Telling the truth also keeps us from telling lies to cover other lies. We no longer have to maintain a list of lies so our stories remain consistent from one telling to the next.

Likewise, just as we should not lie to others, we never should lie to ourselves. If our conscience or our little man in our head is telling us something different from what we are expressing to others, we are lying to ourselves. Not only is it important to be honest with others, we must also be honest with ourselves. If we can't be honest with ourselves, being honest with others will be difficult, if not impossible.

Third, accepting responsibility for our actions and enduring the consequences that result from them is not only the right thing to do, but an indispensable element of telling the truth. We all make mistakes. Errors in judgment are going to happen no matter how hard we try to eliminate them. We must not be tempted to blame someone else when this happens. We must acknowledge our mistakes, learn from them, and accept responsibility and the consequences for our actions.

Fourth, we must always treat others as we want to be treated. If we want people to respect us, we must first respect them. If we want people to value us, we must first show others that they have value. If we want people to treat us a certain way, we must first treat them in the way we want to be treated. We must model to others how we want to be treated.

Finally, living within our means is crucial to living a simple life. We must never put ourselves in a position that requires more resources than we have or have access to. We must evaluate and weigh every purchase before we make it to determine if it is within our financial means and supports our priorities.

Just as important as living within our financial means is to keeping focused on our priorities, we must also live within our time means. As financial means relates to how we spend our money, time means relates to how we budget and spend our time. How we spend our time affects every part of our lives because it is the most valuable resource in the world. Living within our financial and time means assures us that we focus our money and time—our limited resources—on the things that are most important to us.

All five core values work hand in hand to develop a strong belief system. Using these core values help us stay committed to a needs-based lifestyle and evaluate distractions that bombard us daily competing for our resources. They keep our thinking, decisions, and actions in agreement with our beliefs and priorities. Best of all, applying these core values to our lives allows us to live life more simply and find happiness. It allows us to live a life that is a state of uncomplicated, straightforward, unpretentious living, unaffected by worldly desires, wants, or standards, where the focus of our lives is based on our priorities, and the value of our lives is measured by our quality of life, not quantity of life—the simple life.

In the next chapter, we will begin to define your simple life and bring it down from the ten thousand-foot view into the weeds. When you complete this exercise and if you follow the process, your life will have focus and direction it has never had before. I hope you are as excited about your life's new direction as I am. Turn the page and let's get started.

Live the Simple Life You Dream About

We should now have a better understanding of how unrealistic wants influence our life's choices and ultimately our happiness. The creation of unrealistic wants and the perpetuation of them are caused by the lack of satisfaction in our lives. These wants never can be satisfied because the influence of unrealistic wants breeds more unrealistic wants. Once one desire is fulfilled, a new desire is created.

Happiness is the result of being satisfied. In fact, being satisfied is a prerequisite of being happy. Only when we control the influence of unrealistic wants on our lives will we ever find satisfaction with who we are, what we are doing, and where our life is going. However, once we begin to control the influence of unrealistic wants in our lives, happiness quickly follows, our lives get simpler, and the emptiness in our stomach goes away.

When we are unhappy and not satisfied, we sometimes allow the world or circumstances around us to determine the lives we live. Instead of choosing the lifestyle that will bring happiness to our lives, we allow others to decide for us how we live our lives. We allow others to influence our decision making, control our money and time, and clutter our lives with insignificant relationships, activities, and things. When this happens, we redirect our focus away from our priorities and the very things that will bring us happiness. Consequently, we sometimes fall into the lifestyle we lead because of our inability to stay focused on our real needs and priorities.

In 1986, I fell into my career. I didn't choose it. In fact, I had never even heard of it when it chose me. We had just moved to Louisville, Kentucky, and we were deep in debt. We were in the process of losing our home in Franklin, Kentucky, and, quite frankly, everything else we owned. I had two small children and a dedicated wife I pulled along to Louisville in pursuit of greener pastures (we know about greener pastures).

Our move to Louisville, Kentucky, pulled us away from many things we loved. It pulled us away from our home that we fell in love with the moment we first saw it. It was a beautiful home on almost an acre of land within a mile of the city square. It had a great place for the kids to play, a good-sized garden, and even a huge barn out back.

Our move pulled us away from Franklin, Kentucky, a little town two miles inside Kentucky's southern border on Interstate 65. At the time, it was a town of about eight thousand people and a great place to raise a family. This town was so small and close-knit that on my first day in town someone told me, "Chances are you will never be mugged in Franklin, but if you are, you will know who did it." I found that statement to be true. The town seemed like one big family.

We also left behind a wonderful church family and a group of great friends. We were active in First Baptist Church of Franklin, and the friends we met there will always occupy a special place in our hearts. Steve and Leah Atkinson—former Georgia residents—became our best friends on our first Sunday at the church. They were also new in the area, and we bonded the first night we met at an ice cream social.

For the next four years, Steve, Leah, my wife, and I were joined at the hip. We did everything together. They became our family away from our family back in Alabama. If you saw one of us, you saw all of us. We were inseparable. Leaving them to move to Louisville was the hardest thing we ever did, even harder than leaving our parents and siblings in Alabama.

The hope for greener pastures not only pulled us away from all the things we loved about Franklin, it almost cost us everything. Our new jobs in Louisville were not working out, the cost of living was much higher than we anticipated, and our home in Franklin wouldn't sell. Times were tough. We were living outside our means and about to lose everything we held dear.

Looking through the Louisville Sunday newspaper one afternoon, I saw a management position at a large health insurance company that might help my job situation. The job listing didn't describe the job in much detail, but I seemed to have the skills the company was looking for, and it would allow me to work at night—a schedule I needed at the time.

I sent in my resume, and a few days later, I was contacted by the human resources department. To be honest, I was surprised I was contacted so quickly. I had been told all my life that you can't find a good job in the newspaper. Good jobs come through networking with people you know. I was repeatedly told, "It is not what you know, but who you know that gets you hired." I can tell you without hesitation that three of the best jobs I ever held came from contacting companies through a newspaper ad. This is one idea you can eliminate from your belief system.

The interview process was one of the most thorough processes I have ever participated in up to that time. I was interviewed by several people throughout the organization over a two-day period. I was given verbal and written general knowledge tests and managerial situational tests. I was given psychological exams in which I was shown inkblots and had to describe to the interviewer what I saw in each picture. I had never been tested that comprehensively for any job.

During one of the many interviews, I met with my potential boss. She described the position as the manager over the Micrographics Department. Now you may know what this is, but I had no clue. *What is micrographics?* I asked myself.

At first, I was afraid to show my ignorance about the position. I mean, this would surely be the end of the interview, and I would be shown the door if I asked what a micrographics manager does. But as the interview progressed and I felt she was more comfortable with me, I popped the question. "What's micrographics?" As she leaned back in her chair with a slight smirk on her face, she said, "I was wondering when you were going to ask." Get this—they didn't expect me to know about the position. In fact, she said that she would have been shocked if I knew anything about micrographics. She told me the company was looking for a leader, someone who could lead the people of the department. Knowing the technical aspects of the department was secondary to the company. She felt if she could find the right person to lead their employees, management could teach the person they hired the technical aspects of the job.

Within a week or so, I was working at this company as a second shift Micrographics Manager. What does a micrographics manager do? He or she oversees the filming, processing, quality control, and data entry of microfilm. Every document, insurance claim or otherwise, was microfilmed as soon as it entered the mailroom. The microfilm was used to store an image of the original documents as well as route the claims through the insurance claim process for payment. Most companies use scanning technology today, but back then this was high-tech.

If you are anything like me, I thought I had entered into the world of James Bond. Being able to microfilm 3,500 documents and place them on a roll of film that fits in the palm of your hand seemed incredible to me at the time. Little did I know until much later that this company had one of the top ten largest microfilming operations in the United States. To give you an example of how large the company was, I worked directly with equipment design engineers in Japan to develop enhancements to their equipment that became standard features on their later models. We were such a large user of their equipment, they allowed us to work directly with their engineers to develop improvements to their equipment. I can't tell you how many times we had one-of-a-kind prototype devices in our micrographics area conducting beta testing.

The next few years, I learned everything I could and became very knowledgeable about the microfilm process and many other disciplines of records and information management. I invested a lot of energy and worked hard at being the best I could be at this job. In fact, I devised one process improvement that saved the company over one million dollars a year. Even through all of the successes I was having, in the back of my mind, I was not happy. In the pit of my stomach, the job just didn't feel right. In the end, the job never made me happy.

In the late 1980s, my company went through a large downsizing, and although I retained my job when it was over, I asked to leave the company. My boss arranged for me to receive the severance package everyone else was getting, and within a few days I left the company. By this time, my wife had a good job and, financially, my family was more stable. After much discussion, my wife and I felt it was the right thing for me to do.

Because of the experience I gained while there, I found another job in a few weeks. I remained in the records and information management profession for over twenty-seven years. I worked for private industry and government. I worked for health care and even ran a successful consulting business. I earned two certifications that combined, fewer than twenty people hold worldwide. I became an expert in the records and information management field and was well respected by my peers. But even through the experience I gained, the certifications I acquired, and the respect I was given in the industry, I was still not happy. Though I couldn't put a finger on why I was unhappy at the time, I felt empty inside.

How can a career that has spanned over twenty-seven years leave me feeling unhappy, unfulfilled? After much self-reflection, I concluded that it is because I wasn't doing what I love. I wasn't working at the things I love to do or focusing my time and energy on the things that were important to me. I didn't choose this career because I loved it. I chose it because I needed a job, and it paid the bills. You know what they say, "If you work doing what you love to do, you never work another day in your life." That's where I messed up. I didn't choose to live life doing what I loved, and it left me empty inside.

Don't get me wrong, records and information management is a great profession. It allowed me to put two children through college without borrowing a single dime. It allowed me to travel the world and see and do things I wouldn't have otherwise done. It provided me with a lot of trusted friends and associates throughout the world. However, even after you add up all the benefits of being in this profession, it still didn't make me happy. Although I spent over twenty-seven years working hard to learn everything I could, doing the best job I could do for whomever I worked, and providing a stable income and security for my family, I never felt satisfied, never completely happy.

In retrospect, it shouldn't have taken me twenty-seven years to figure out the emptiness I felt inside my gut. I should have stopped and evaluated my life much sooner than I did. I let the influence of unrealistic wants in my life choose my life for me. I let the security of a good-paying, steady job influence my decisions about how I lived my life. I let the influence of unrealistic wants in my life coerce me into staying in a career that didn't make me happy. Although I had the financially secure life everyone hopes to have, I felt empty inside and unhappy with the path my life was taking.

I can only assume that if you are reading this book, you are where I was several years ago. To put it simply, I was not happy. Although my life, financially and in every other respect was almost perfect, I felt an emptiness in my stomach. In fact, if you can understand this logic, I was so unhappy that until I started investigating why I was unhappy, I didn't realize how truly unhappy I was. The emptiness I felt was beginning to control my every thought.

In the depths of my despair, I decided to do something about it. The process I am going to share with you in the remaining pages of this book is the result of my search to fill that void in my life and find the real happiness I was looking for.

Why was I so unhappy? At the end of the process, I discovered that my unhappiness came from choosing to live a lifestyle that didn't incorporate my life's priorities and the things I love to do. I let the stresses of life distract me from the things that were most important to me. Instead of choosing the lifestyle that incorporated all the things I love, I let life choose me and allowed it to form the lifestyle I ultimately led. As I found out, real happiness comes from surrounding yourself with the people, activities, and things you love and living your life focused on these things. Perhaps Ben Stiller, who played the character of Larry Daley in the movie *Night at the Museum: Battle of the Smithsonian*, said it best: "The key to true happiness is doing the things you love with the people you love."[29]

But more than discovering what true happiness is, being happy is a process. It doesn't happen haphazardly. True happiness comes through, as Larry Daley would say, defining the people you love and the things you love to do and making them a priority in your life.

I think the simple life, as I have defined it, is our ultimate goal. It is living a life that is a state of uncomplicated, straightforward, unpretentious living, unaffected by worldly desires, wants, or standards, where the focus of our lives is based on our priorities, and the value of our lives is measured by our quality of life, not quantity of life—the simple life.

I know you're probably thinking to yourself, *Who wouldn't want to live that life. But, Bobby, how do I bring your high-level definition or view of the simple life down to something I can apply to my life?* I'm glad you asked. Continue to read my book and my blog at www.SimpleLifePublishing.com, and I will lead you down the path to finding the life that, up until now, you have only dreamed about.

In the past several pages of the previous chapter, we defined the key components of our core-value system and discussed the benefits. Now it is time to start weighing our decisions, actions, and priorities against these values. Focusing on these core values as we live our lives helps us eliminate the distractions that surround us and helps keep us focused on the people we love and the things we love to do. Only when we are able to eliminate the influence of these distractions are we able to keep our lives focused on our priorities.

How do we apply the core values to our lives? Here is where we begin to simplify our lives. Every decision we make should be weighed against our core values. If the decision we are considering doesn't agree with our "always do the right thing" value, we make a decision that does. If we are about to tell a whopper that has measured consequences, we tell the truth. If we are about to make excuses and blame someone else for something we did, we use our third core value and accept responsibility for our actions. If we are considering treating someone in a way that doesn't agree with our value of "treating people as we would want to be treated," we don't do it. If we are about to make a purchase and it doesn't meet our "live within our means" value, we don't buy it. If we are about to make a commitment to an activity that we don't have time for or that will distract us from our priorities, we decline gracefully. The process of incorporating the five core values into our lives is as simple as I have just explained.

My son is a rocket scientist—he really is—and this concept is not rocket science. As simple as this may sound, with practice, these core values will hopefully become the driving force in our lives. Used together, these core values will help us stay focused on our priorities. When we remain focused on our priorities, we simplify our lives and allow ourselves to find true, sustaining happiness.

To live the simple life we dream about, we must go through a process. Everything in life is a process. It doesn't happen by chance. It happens because of a process a person follows to become successful at whatever he or she chooses to be successful doing. Following the process makes success possible.

What kind of process am I talking about? I'm talking about the same kind of process children go through to learn to run. They don't learn to run at the exact moment they are born. They learn to run by going through a process. First, they learn to scoot on their bellies, rock back and forth on their knees, and crawl across the floor. Only after they go through this process and learn these skills, can they learn to stand up by holding onto the couch or a chair. The process progresses from there to children taking their first steps toward their moms or dads. Eventually, they let go of the sofa and walk a few steps into their parents' outstretched arms. Only then, do they begin to learn to run. With encouragement from their parents, children let go of the couch. They slowly loosen their fingers from their death-grip on the sofa, and, with the courage of a lion, run as fast as they can from the couch to a nearby chair. With time, they run freely without any assistance from their parents or the living room furniture. With additional time, some children grow up through other processes, to become championship runners.

Likewise, making the ultimate chocolate chip cookie is the result of a process.[30] A procedure must be followed to make them taste just right. First, we have to take three-fourths of a cup of granulated sugar, three-fourths of a cup of packed brown sugar, one cup of butter, one teaspoon of vanilla, one egg, two and a fourth cups of Gold Medal® all-purpose flour, one teaspoon of baking soda, a half teaspoon of salt, one cup of coarsely chopped nuts, and twelve ounces or two cups of semisweet chocolate chips and mix them all together in a bowl.

Do we just throw all the ingredients into the bowl and mix them up? No, we first mix the sugars, butter, vanilla, and egg—in this order—and then slowly mix in the flour, baking soda, and the salt. As the mixture begins to stiffen, we add the nuts and finally the chocolate chips.

Are we finished? Of course not; we must now preheat the oven to 375^0 F and drop rounded tablespoons of dough about two inches apart onto an ungreased cookie sheet. Once the oven beeps to let us know it has reached the prescribed temperature, we place the cookie sheet into the oven, close the door, and let the dough bake for eight to ten minutes or until the dough is light brown.

When they are just right, we remove the cookies from the oven and the cookie sheet and let them cool on a wire rack. Once cool, we eat them as fast as we can before the smell of the cookies draws everyone in the house to the kitchen. We know from past experience that it may be our only chance to get a cookie before they are all gone.

While you're eating your freshly made cookies, think about this idea for a moment: everything in life is defined by a process. From simple processes such as the routine we follow each morning to get dressed for work, to putting a man on the moon, each accomplishment is achieved through a well-defined process. It only stands to reason that, if we follow the process, we increase our odds of being successful at whatever we are attempting to do. Isn't that what life is all about—being successful doing the things we want to do?

As these examples clearly illustrate, every success story in life is the result of a process—a step-by-step procedure, if you will, that must be followed to ensure success. The direction our lives ultimately take is no different. To live the simple life and find the true happiness we are seeking, like everything we do, we must follow a process.

The process to live the simple life you dream about has five major steps. In the first step, we reduced or eliminated outside influences on our decision making by developing a strong core-value system. We must learn to listen only to the voice that comes from within our hearts and use it to guide us in the choices we need to make about how we live our lives. This step of the process is important in helping us understand what we really need to be happy. Developing a strong core-value system, the process we just finished discussing, allows us to evaluate the distractions that bombard us daily and compete for our resources. Having a strong core-value system keeps our thinking, decisions, and actions in agreement with our beliefs and our priorities.

In the second step, we must define our priorities. We must identify the people, activities, and things that are important to us, that bring satisfaction and meaning to our lives. Once we define our priorities, we must stay close to them. We must incorporate them into the very fabric our lives. At the same time we define our priorities, we must ascertain where we are at this point in our lives and determine where we want our lives to go in the future. We must define and establish tangible goals that we can commit to and work toward.

In the third step of the process, we must develop a solid money-management plan. Living within our means is one of the most important factors determining our happiness. Keeping our spending under control helps keep us on track and removes many of the daily distractions that challenge our efforts at living the lives we want to live. It also allows us to reallocate our funds to support our priorities and goals in a more meaningful way.

Likewise, just as we need to develop a solid money-management plan, in step four, we must also establish a plan to manage our time more efficiently. We have only twenty-four hours a day to live our lives. Once these twenty-four hours are spent, they can never be recovered. They are gone forever. With this plan, we evaluate our time needs and identify places where we can reallocate our resources to ensure we are spending time on the people, activities, things, and goals that are important to us.

In the fifth and final step of the process, we must declutter our lives. We must remove all of the distractions—both physical and emotional—from our lives that keep us from our priorities. These distractions, if we allow them to control us, will suck the life out of us and prevent us from living the lives we dream about. We must take constructive steps to eliminate these distractions from our lives to free up resources—both money and time—that can be used to support our priorities and goals.

Dedicating yourself to this process will change your life forever. Just as it did with me, maybe for the first time you will understand how to live your life to the fullest. As the process dictates, to be truly happy, you must first determine what gives meaning to your life. Next, you must develop a plan incorporating all the things that are important to you into your lifestyle with the resources needed to support them. Finally, you must eliminate the clutter that sometimes gets in the way of living the life you dream about. When you follow this process, life is simpler and true happiness comes naturally.

Step Two: Defining Our Priorities

Defining our priorities is the second step in the process of living the simple life you dream about. In this step of the process, we want to determine and identify what is important to us. What are our priorities? Who are the people, activities, or things in our lives that we cannot live without? Identifying the priorities that give meaning to our lives is our goal.

According to the *Encarta Dictionary*, priority means "the state of having the most importance or urgency, somebody or something that is ranked highly in terms of importance, and/or the right to be ranked above others."[31] In short, a priority means what is most important. In the context of this exercise, a priority is defined as what is most important to you.

There are several categories from which you could pull your priorities. Family, work, friends, religion, sports, and hobbies—just to name a few—may all hold a special place in your heart. Focus your effort on the things most important to you, that you consider a priority in your life.

Look at it this way: if you had all the time and money in the world, what would you do with your time and how would you spend your money? Who are the people you want to spend time with? Who are the people you want in your life? What activities make you the happiest? What things in your life give you the most joy?

If you're still confused about what we are trying to identify in this step of the process, maybe looking at it from the opposite perspective will help. What if you didn't have all the time and money in the world? What if you had only one month to live—how would this realization change your life? How would you spend your remaining days? Who are the people you would spend your remaining time with? What activities or things would you move to the top of your priority list and focus on? Does this perspective help? These are the people, activities, and things we are trying to identify with the following exercises.

In the next several pages, we are going to go through a process to determine the priorities in our lives. Now, I realize this exercise may be a difficult task for some of us. Some of us have never taken the time out of our busy lives to think about and organize the things in our lives that should be a priority. It was difficult for me the first time I did it.

However, as I said before, I can only assume that if you are reading this book, something in your life is missing. You don't smile as widely as you once did. The spring in your step is not as high as it used to be. You're not as happy as you once were. Now is the time to refocus your energy and resources. Now is the time to reflect on your life and identify the people, activities, and things that make you happy.

You deserve to be happy. Remember what we said earlier about happiness? True happiness is doing the things you love with the people you love. Defining your priorities is the next step to finding the real happiness you're seeking.

Don't get discouraged if it takes you several lists or brainstorming sessions to determine your final list of priorities. When I made my first list, I kept writing down items that were not necessarily my priorities. I kept thinking that, because it was important to someone else, it should be a priority in my life too. I kept thinking in the back of my head that it should be a priority even though it really wasn't.

Remember the distractions we talked about in an earlier chapter? These distractions kept drawing my focus away from the things that were most important to me, my priorities. They kept finding their way on my list when I knew in my heart that they shouldn't be there. Try not to let these same distractions influence your list of priorities. The priorities you are defining during these exercises are yours and yours alone.

Once you establish your list of priorities, unless you share them with someone else, it will never be seen by anyone but you. Remember, you are the only one you are trying to make happy. Therefore, be honest with yourself. Don't let distractions or outside influences sway your decisions about your lists. You are the only person you must answer to. If you can't be honest with yourself, who can you be honest with, right?

When we define the priorities that will be the focal point of our lives, I think there are four main areas we must focus on to get to the heart of the matter. There may be others, and if you think there are, please share your ideas with me. I want to hear from you. To me, the four main areas that are important in establishing our priorities are important people, goals or things we want to do, things we should be doing that we're not doing, and a catchall area called things or stuff that make us happy. Priorities from these four areas build a strong foundation for what should be important in our lives.

For the remainder of this chapter, we will work together to identify your priorities in each area. As we review each area, I will describe to you what we are looking for so your simple life foundation can be built to withstand the test of time.

To be honest, some of the decisions we will need to make during this process will be difficult. Setting priorities, especially life priorities, is never easy. However, don't get discouraged. Stick with the process. The process works. The list of priorities we create will start the process of determining our life's direction and allow us to find the true happiness we are looking for.

The first list we must create is our Important People Priority List.

Priority List One: Important People

For the next few minutes, I want us to think about all the people in our lives we would consider a priority. Who are the people that mean the most to our lives and are important to our well-being? Who are the people we want to be around constantly? Which people are the pillars of our lives and the ones who give our lives meaning? Over the next several minutes, I want us to identify these people and evaluate their importance to us.

Some of the people we think about will be obvious. A spouse of thirty years, a parent, a child, or a best friend is easy to identify. All these people hold a special place in our hearts because of our relationship to them.

In contrast, some of the people who come to mind may not hold a special place in our lives now, but we know they should. Maybe it is an old friend we've distanced ourselves from and let slip away. Maybe it is a family member that for whatever reason we are at odds with and we have not always been there for them. It could even be a spouse, boyfriend, or girlfriend we have lost touch with, and the relationship is not what it used to be. Whatever the reason, we know these people should be a priority in our lives, but right now, they're not.

Our ultimate goal is to identify all the people we want to have a major role in our lives. These people are the surest way to our happiness. These are the people we want in our lives, no matter what the cost. These are the people we are trying to identify with this list.

For the next few minutes, take a piece of paper and write down all the names of the people you want to be a priority in your life. Spend a few moments in a quiet place without distractions and think about the people who make you happy and bring a smile to your face. Reflect on the people who are important to you that you would do anything for. Think about the people who may not be in your life now, but should be. As soon as you think of someone, write down his or her name. Try not to analyze your list at this point. We'll do that later. For now, as soon as you think of someone, write his or her name down and move on. Once you think you have a good list, put it in a safe place, and we will try to make sense of it later.

How did it go? Did you have trouble coming up with your list of important people? As unbelievable as this may sound, some of you will have written down a hundred names or more. Every inch of the paper may be filled with names of your family, friends, and acquaintances. That's okay. Although your list may seem overwhelming right now, we will refine it later and make it manageable.

Just as some of you had hundreds of names on your final list, some of you will have struggled to come up with even a few names. Please don't let this discourage you. Keep working on your list. Take as much time as you need to get your list of names together. Once your juices get flowing, you will start to identify the people who are important to you.

Although this exercise is fairly straightforward, some of us will better understand what we are trying to accomplish if we can see what others have written on their lists. Some of us are just wired that way. We have to see what others are thinking to get our juices flowing. To assist us, I have created a fictitious couple—John and Kristina Pennywise—who will share their results of each exercise with us.

However, don't let what they have chosen influence your final lists. You are creating priority lists unique to you. Don't let John's, Kristina's, or anyone else's priorities influence what's important to you in any way.

So what did John and Kristina write down on their Important People Priority List? They worked on their lists separately and shared them with each other only when their lists were complete. They followed this process throughout every priority list exercise. If you are completing these exercises with someone else, you may want to consider their approach. I think using this approach helps reduce the impact of outside influences on your final list. In the end, whether or not you share your lists with your partner is up to you.

Here are a few examples of the important people John and Kristina wrote on their priority lists:

John

- Kristina
- Mother
- Father
- Sister Paula
- Brother Bobby
- Grandfather
- Best Friend Tom
- Jeff at work

Kristina

- John
- Father
- Mother

- Best Friend Teresa
- Charlie Her Brother
- Jayne a Former College School Friend
- Best Friend LaDonna
- Penny at Church
- Uncle Josh

Does this help? Did seeing what John and Kristina wrote down help you focus on the important people in your life? We all have important people in our lives who give our lives meaning and make us happy. Completing this exercise helps us define who they are so we can give them the attention they deserve.

Defining the important people in your life is the first step in understanding your priorities. It is important that you take time to list the people who you want to have a major part in your life. If you are going to enjoy the true happiness that comes through living a simple life, you must invest the time needed to identify the people you want surrounding you.

If you haven't already, spend time now writing down all the important people who you want to be in your life. I promise I will change your life with this list later. When you have completed your list, go to the next section: goals or things I want to do.

Priority List Two: Things I Want To Do

Welcome back to the book! At this point you should have at least started your priority list of important people. You may not have your final list, but hopefully you understand what we are trying to accomplish, and you can keep adding names to your list until you are happy with it.

To be honest, as time goes by and as we mature in life, our priorities change. Everybody's does. From time to time, we will need to reevaluate our priorities and update our priority lists to keep our lists in agreement with where we are at that point in our lives.

For now, put your Important People Priority List to the side, and let's work on our next list. On the second list, we want to identify the things we want to do but never had or made the time to accomplish.

We all have things we want to do catalogued in the "someday" part of our minds. We say things like, "I don't have time right now. I'm too busy with my job, family obligations, school, game system, or (insert your reason here) to do it right now." Or we say things like, "I just don't have the money, educational background, experience, free time, courage, or (insert your reason here) to make it happen." For whatever reason, we put off these things and never get around to doing them.

Oh, we try to make it sound like we have a real plan we're following. Some of us call our list of things we want to do someday a "bucket list." This list includes all the things we say we want to do before we die. Whether this list is an actual list of things to do or a list of things still floating around lost in the someday part of our minds, calling it a bucket list gives us some comfort that we are at least pretending to do something about our future goals. However, unless we are actively working toward doing something on our bucket list, this is just another excuse we use to put off doing something we really want to do.

Why do we do this? Why do we put things off and never get around to doing the things we really want to do? Why do we say we are going to wait until just before we die before we do anything about it?

The reason we put our lives on hold is because we don't have a plan. We've never stopped long enough to devise a plan so we know how to get from where we are now to where we want to be. To put it bluntly, we must stop talking about all the things we want to do and start doing something about them. I know you're probably tired of me saying this, but life is too short. It is time for us to get up off our collective duffs, start making plans about our future, and free up our time and resources to accomplish all the things we dream about doing someday.

Your plan starts with the list of things you want to do. What am I looking for here? This list can include anything you want to achieve. It doesn't have to be something big like becoming the president of the United States. It can be something as small as not closing your hand in the door when you let the dog in from outside. It doesn't have to be something that costs three trillion dollars to do. It can be something that doesn't cost anything, such as stopping yourself from picking your nose in public. Anything you've put off doing, never focused on accomplishing, or relegated to the "someday" part of your mind is eligible for this list. The examples I provided give you a wide range of things that could make your priority list.

Writing a book about this process was one of the things on my priority list. It is something I put off for years. Not until I committed it to my list, made a plan, and started freeing up resources to make it happen, did it become a reality. Just like my dreams, your dreams can become a reality too. Stay with me through this process, and I will help you devise a plan to make all your dreams come true.

The point of this exercise is to help you move anything you have wanted to do from the "someday" part of your mind into an action plan. This list may include trips you have always wanted to take, a course at the local community college you are interested in, or a hobby that seems fun or appealing. Or it could be something much more substantial such as changing your career path by looking for a new job or moving to a beach resort town. And, yes, it could include becoming the president of the United States. Whatever it is, if there is something you have always dreamed about, but never made the time to do, spend time now and write it down.

Here are five things John and Kristina put on their Things I Want to Do List:

John

- Get an MBA
- Learn to Scuba Dive
- Change Jobs
- Go to the NCAA Basketball Tourney
- Take My Dad to a NASCAR Race

Kristina

- Learn to Play the Guitar
- Go to Rome
- Learn to Scuba Dive
- Change My Hair Color and Style
- Write a Cookbook

Did you notice that both John and Kristina wanted to learn to scuba dive? Not until they went though this simple exercise did they realize their partner wanted to make this activity a priority in their life. Up until now, it had only been something they had talked about doing someday. Now that they have identified it as a priority in their lives, they can begin to commit to and assign resources to accomplishing their goal. I'll show you how to do this later in the book.

What does this list accomplish? It helps us commit to things we want to do. It provides solid goals we can prioritize and allocate resources to accomplish. It takes the goals from the "someday" part of our minds and moves them into action.

Once you have your Goals or Things I Want to Do List completed, put it in a safe place with your Important People Priority List, and we will come back to both lists once all our priority lists are finished.

Priority List Three: Things I Should Be Doing

Although I think this exercise is fairly straightforward on what we are trying to identify, let me provide a few examples. Obviously, we need to spend more time with the important people in our lives, start working toward achieving our goals, and eliminating the things that are wasting our resources, but this list is much more than that. This priority list is intended to help us identify, through personal reflection, all the things we have put off doing for whatever reason. Instead of listing goals or things we want to accomplish, as we did in the previous list, this list is for identifying things we have intentionally blocked from our minds and avoided, even though we know we shouldn't. Does this help?

Let me offer a few illustrations of what we are looking for that will bring this exercise down to earth. There are very few Americans who don't need to lose a little weight. For whatever reason, we have put it off. We know we shouldn't, but we do. Now is the time to write this down on our priority list and make it a priority in our lives.

Take our eating habits as an example. I'll go into this particular subject in much more detail in a later book, but think about this for a moment. Instead of the normal diet plans and gimmicks marketed to us, what if we based our eating habits on the simple lifestyle formula and ate only what we needed? Instead of counting this or that as some plans suggest, we eat only what we need—what is necessary—to meet our baseline satisfaction needs. Sticking to the simple lifestyle formula, over time will allow our bodies to naturally gravitate to our normal weight and body shape programmed into our DNA. In the end, we may not be as skinny as a supermodel or have muscles like Mr. Olympus, but by taking this approach, our bodies will be allowed to find their natural shapes and sizes. Instead of living to eat, we eat to live.

Another example of things we should be doing may be to spend more time with a sick friend or a relative we have distanced ourselves from. Sometimes, avoidable and unavoidable things happen that tear us away from people who once held a special place in our heart. Unfortunately, it sometimes takes a life-changing event to make us realize how important this person is to us. Perhaps there is someone in our lives who fits this description with whom we need to bury the hatchet and ask back into our lives. Don't wait any longer, write it down on this list and make it a priority.

We could come up with hundreds of examples, things we have put off too long. Maybe we need to reconnect with a parent whom we have distanced ourselves from. Maybe we need to make amends with someone we have purposely excluded from our lives. Maybe we need to get involved in church and become more active again. Whatever we have been deliberately avoiding, write it down. Now is the time to focus on these things and make them a priority in our lives.

The major goal of this priority list is to provide personal growth and enrichment in our lives. This list helps us tie up loose ends, clears our conscience of undone things, and enhances our satisfaction as we start to accomplish the things we have been avoiding.

One word of caution: don't let the outside influences we have been talking about affect what you write down. Remember how these influences try to sway how we think and act? There were many things on my original list that I thought I should be doing, but deep down I wasn't motivated to do. I had to stop and evaluate my motivation on each item. I had to determine whether I was thinking I should do it because of my own needs or because I was letting the needs of someone else influence my decision. After much soul searching, I decided that if I thought I was being influenced by someone else's need for me to do something, it didn't make my final list. I ignored it. Here's why: if we let others influence our decisions about how we live our lives, we will never be completely happy.

Here are four things John and Kristina put on their Things I Know I Should Be Doing List:

John

- Lose Weight
- Reassign or Terminate Frank
- Apologize to My Best Friend
- Stop Watching So Much TV

Kristina

- Lose Weight
- Volunteer at the Church
- Quit Spending So Much Money on Shoes
- Change Doctors

Notice again that John and Kristina both put down losing weight as a priority on their lists. They are lucky in the sense that they have someone to share this goal with to help distribute the load of staying committed.

This priority list helps remove the burden of guilt from our conscience and makes it easier for us to find happiness. Spend some time now looking deep within yourself through your list of things you have been avoiding. Once you have a good list, set it to the side in a safe place with the other priority lists you have made so far. Once we finish the final priority list, you and I will pull all the lists together and build the foundation of your simple life.

Priority List Four: Things That Make Me Happy

The fourth and final priority list we need to create is our Things That Make Me Happy List. On this catchall list, we want to write down everything that makes us happy. This list has no boundaries. It could be a special place or city. It could be a sport you like to participate in or watch. It could be your favorite restaurant or food. It could be a special activity that stimulates you. Whatever it is, if it makes you happy, write it down on this list.

For me, besides all the normal things like my family, friends, and macaroni and cheese, there are three major things that get me excited about life and bring me happiness. The first thing is Alabama Crimson Tide football. I love it. I like following the team, watching the games, and tracking player development. I love observing the excitement of the fans when the Tide scores a touchdown. I love the tradition of the program and all the famous coaches and players who have made their mark on history. I love Alabama football so much that I created a blog site called Tide Tradition several years ago so I could share my excitement with others. You can find it at www.TideTradition.com. I hope you will check it out and join with me in the fun.

The second thing that brings me happiness is writing. I love to write. Even more than putting the words on the page, I like the creative side of writing. I am happiest when I'm in front of a computer being creative. Once I finally realized how happy it made me, I started writing my first book, *The Building Blocks of Success: Focus On the Fundamentals and Be Successful at Everything You Do*. In my book, I break down the process of being successful into its seven fundamental elements. In essence, I try to simplify the process of being successful so the reader can be successful at everything he or she attempts. I show, through stories about my children, that we already have all the skills we need to be successful, and if we make these seven fundamental elements a priority in everything we do, success comes naturally.

The third thing that brings me happiness is helping people follow their dreams. We all have dreams. We all have things we want to do, but for some reason we never commit to them. I used to be the same way. I liked helping others follow their dreams, but I never followed my own. One day it hit me that I needed to start taking my own advice and help myself. Because of that epiphany and my desire to help people follow their dreams, I started the company Simple Life Publishing and a blog site (www.SimpleLifePublishing.com) to share my ideas. This site allows me to follow my dream and do something that makes me happy at the same time. As part of this same goal, I wrote my second book—you guessed it—the book you're reading now.

All the examples I've just given you of the things that make me happy started with the simple lifestyle process we are talking about now. Each one was written on my list of Things That Make Me Happy priority list. Not until I wrote them on my list, went through the process I am teaching you now, and made them a priority in my life, did any of the things I listed happen. In fact, not until I committed to all the people, activities, and things listed on my four priority lists was I able to simplify my life and find the true happiness that comes from it. I want you to find the true happiness I found. I promise that if you stay with me, I will get you there too.

Here are a few things that John and Kristina wrote down on their Things That Make Me Happy List:

John

- Strawberry Ice Cream
- Alabama Football
- NASCAR Racing
- The Beach
- Hiking in the Woods
- Watching Sports on TV
- Writing
- Being with My Wife
- Listening to Shortwave Radio
- Hunting

Kristina

- Dressing Up and Going out on the Town
- Eating at a Nice Restaurant
- Chocolate Chip Cookies
- The Mall
- Cooking
- Hanging out with Friends
- Staying in a Cabin in the Mountains
- Swimming

- Riding My Bicycle
- Singing in the Shower

John and Kristina had few problems writing things on this list. This list is fun to create because it allows us to identify and write down everything that makes us happy and puts a smile on our faces.

Spend a few minutes now and think about the places, things, and activities that make you happy. It doesn't have to be something as big as starting a blog site or writing a book. It can be anything that puts a smile on your face or puts a little extra spring in your step. It could be a place you lived or visited that holds a special place in your heart. It could be something you like to spend your time doing. It could be something as simple as your favorite ice cream. Let your mind run wild. Spend all the time you need, and write down all the things that make you happy—the things that get you excited about life!

Were you surprised at what you wrote down? I know I was when I first defined my list of things that make me happy. There were things on my list that I would never show to anyone, not even my wife. There were things on my list that I later removed. There were things on my list that I didn't consciously know made me happy until I thought about it. There were things that made me laugh, things that made me cry—in a happy way, things that required further evaluation, and things that I knew would change my life significantly if I followed through on them and made them a priority in my life.

Once your list is finished, put it with your other priority lists in a safe place. Next, we will start pulling the priority lists together and making sense out of what you've written down.

Making Sense out of Our Priority Lists

Throughout this chapter we have been creating our priority lists. Now it is time to organize our lists and turn them into something we can use to refocus our lives and find true happiness.

At this point, you should have the following four lists:
1) Important People Priority List
2) Things I Want to Do Priority List
3) Things I Should Be Doing Priority List
4) Things That Make Me Happy Priority List

Simple Life Target

I could have had you create your priority lists in any order, but I purposely had you create them in the order I think makes the most sense. As the illustration depicts, think of your four priority lists as a target with your Important People Priority List as the bull's-eye. View each successive list as a separate ring in the target, with your Things I Should Be Doing Priority List as the outside ring. Imagine the Things That Make Me Happy Priority List as the target area outside of the rings. Visualize your Things That Make Me Happy Priority List as the place where all the rings—your priority lists—are allowed to exist. If you will, envision your Things That Make Me Happy List as the glue that holds all the rings in place. Without this important list, the other lists or rings of the target don't exist.

Like any game or sport that uses a target, the objective of the game is to hit the target and stay as close to the center of the bulls'-eye as possible. The target of your four priority lists we just constructed is no different. Our goal is to hit the target and stay as close to our priorities as possible. Remember, real happiness comes from doing the things we love with the people we love.

The target listing all of our priorities is a visual representation of the foundation we are building for our simple life or, as I sometimes like to call it, our Simple Life Plan. Focusing our energy and resources on our simple life target is our basis for happiness.

Here is how our target of priorities works: if we live our lives on the target, first, we stay close to the people who mean the most to us and whom we want in our lives. Second, we begin to make the things we want to do a priority and start to accomplish all the things we keep putting off. Third, we begin to do the things we know we should be doing that will bring meaning and value to our lives. Finally, we surround ourselves and our priorities with all the things that make us happy and make life worth living. Our four priority lists work together to help us find true happiness. In addition to finding true happiness, making our four lists a priority in our lives simplifies our lives by keeping our important things close to us and letting everything else go.

Although our priority lists represent the things that are important to us at this moment in time, please remember that our Simple Life Plan is not a static plan. It is a living, breathing plan that must be reviewed and updated occasionally. As we grow older and our lives change, our plan must be updated to reflect the things that are most important in our lives at that particular point in our journey. I suggest that we review our priority lists at least every six months. For some of us, it will be necessary to review our lists every quarter or maybe every month. How often you review and update your Simple Life Plan is up to you. The important thing is that we take time to do it. Doing so will help us keep focused on the important things in our lives.

At this point you may be asking yourself, *Okay, I have four lists that represent the priorities of the simple life I am trying to create for myself. How do I use them?* Use your lists as your life centering focus on how you want to live your life. When you created your priority lists, you identified all the people, activities, and things in your life that are important to you. You identified all the things you are avoiding that will bring meaning back into your life. With this new knowledge, you must incorporate all the things that are important to you—the people, activities, and things—into your everyday life and discard everything else. Throw them away. Get rid of them. Doing otherwise will only lead you to unhappiness, frustration, and an emptiness in your life that you will never be able to fill.

The next step of the process is to come out of the conceptual cloud and go down into the weeds to incorporate our four priority lists into our daily living. Now that we understand the concept of living a simple life, we can start applying the concept to our everyday living.

Incorporating Our Four Priority Lists into Our Daily Living

Let's focus on your priority lists and start with the bull's-eye of your target, your Important People Priority List. This list identifies the people in your life who are most important to you—the people you want to be around and spend time with, the people you want to grow old with and have as an active participant in your life. Always keep these people close. They should always be above everyone else in your life. These people are important guiding forces in your life and help you keep centered and on track. These people are of utmost importance in your Simple Life Plan.

The Things I Want to Do Priority List or the second ring of your Simple Life Plan represents the things you have put off or never made time to do—the things you dream about. They are the "someday" or the "if I only had time" things in your life. You know in your heart that if you make time for these things, they will make you happy and bring satisfaction to your life. You must always make time for the things on this list. They represent the unfulfilled dreams of your life. They have the greatest opportunity to bring you contentment and happiness.

The Things I Should Be Doing Priority List, or third ring of your Simple Life Plan, contains the things you have been avoiding. You know without a doubt your life would benefit from doing these things, but for whatever reason the perceived benefits have never moved you into action. Making the items on this list a priority reduces your guilty conscience and improves your overall outlook on life. Even though you know that you may not see an immediate benefit with these items, over time you know they will greatly enhance your life if you only tackle them and make them a part of your daily living. You must find the time and motivation to accomplish the items on this list. Ultimately, these items could give you great satisfaction.

The final list of your Simple Life Plan is your Things That Make Me Happy Priority List, which is the glue that holds everything together. These are the things in your life that make you happy. These are the special places, activities, or things that put a smile on your face or a spring in your step, the things that bring joy to your life. You must incorporate the items on this list throughout your life at every opportunity.

Everything on this priority list should be combined with every other list you have in your Simple Life Plan to enhance your living. For example, if one of the items on your Things That Make You Happy Priority List is chocolate ice cream, spend time with one of your most important people at your local ice cream store. If hiking is on your happy list, and one of the items on your Things I Should Be Doing Priority List is exercising more, design your exercise program around hiking.

The same is true of the items on your Things I Should Be Doing Priority List. Do things on this list while incorporating something on your Things That Make Me Happy Priority List. Whatever your task, incorporate the things you like to do into the activity. Let's say you have an employee who is not working out, and you have been avoiding confronting him. Take him for ice cream to discuss his shortcomings and devise a corrective plan. Or take him on a hike around the block while you counsel his performance. Just as you can use your happy list to enhance the things you want to do and make it a more enjoyable experience, you can use the things that make you happy to alleviate the heartburn of the things you don't like to do.

For my wife, it's exercising. She hates it. Although she knows its benefits, she avoided it—until she combined her love of reading with her daily workout. Now she rides a recumbent bicycle in our local gym every morning while she reads her favorite book. Not until she starting combining the thing she absolutely loves to do with something she put off doing, did she start exercising regularly. Now, she rides her bike and reads her book every day. In just over three months, she feels better and has lost over thirty-five pounds.

In simplest terms, connect all your priority lists. Use them together and allow them to complement one another. When the priority lists work together, they help you stay focused on all of your priorities. The ultimate goal in this process would be to combine things on all four priority lists at the same time and let them work together to keep you focused on finding the simple life and the happiness you are pursuing.

By incorporating your priority lists into your daily living, you take the second step in creating your Simple Life Plan and can now start living life paying attention to the things most important to you, the people, activities, and things that bring you happiness. You can avoid all the distractions in life that steal your time, energy, and money by focusing your life on the things that make life worth living.

Happiness comes from surrounding ourselves with and focusing our resources on the things that are most important to us and from eliminating everything that distracts us from our priorities. By creating our four priority lists, we have identified the things that are important to us and have started to create our Simple Life Plan—a state of uncomplicated, straightforward, unpretentious living, unaffected by worldly desires, wants, or standards, where the focus of our lives is based on our priorities, and the value of our life is measured by our quality of life, not quantity of life. This lifestyle is not influenced by others or by life's circumstances, but is a lifestyle designed by us and for us through the priorities we choose to focus on.

At times it may be necessary for us to prioritize items within a priority list. Some of the priority lists we created may be large. Experts say that a person's ideal span of control is about five to seven items.[32] For example, if we have one hundred people on our Important People Priority List, we probably have too many people to incorporate effectively into our lives. We need to prioritize the names on our list so that the most important people are at the top. Once they are prioritized, we must focus our energy and resources on the top five to seven people for us to be most effective and to give ourselves the most satisfaction.

Now, I am not saying that our span of control can't be larger than seven. Some people are better at multitasking than others. However, five to seven seems to be the ideal span of control that allows us to keep a good handle on everything we're trying to focus on. This span of control should be applied to all four priority lists in our Simple Life Plan. In addition, reprioritizing our lists from time to time will help us stay focused on our most important people, activities, and things as items are added or removed from our lists.

Staying focused on our Simple Life Plan is the key to our happiness. Everything we need to make us happy is in our four priority lists. Everything we need to bring fulfillment to our life is organized into easily understandable lists. Everything that is important to us is clearly identified and is waiting for us to take action.

Take the four priority lists you created and make them the focal point of your life. Take control of your life today with your priority lists, and live life the way that makes you happy and gives you the most satisfaction.

Although defining our priority lists and living our lives according to what is important to us is critical to finding true happiness, it is only the second step of our Simple Life Plan. Establishing our resources requirements—financial and time—needed to support our priorities is the next step of the process. Turn the page and let's get started.

Step Three: Establishing Our Financial Means

Now that we have defined our life's priorities, it is time to concentrate on our financial resources and establish the next piece of our Simple Life Plan, our Financial Means Plan.

What is a Financial Means Plan? Our Financial Means Plan is our money management strategy that helps us stay focused on the things that are most important to us. Just as our priority lists identify and organize all the people, activities, and things that are the basis for our happiness, our Financial Means Plan establishes our money management objectives to keep us on track with our Simple Life Plan.

In the next few pages, we are going to establish our financial means. Through the exercises that follow, we will determine our spending habits and our baseline budget requirements and develop a budget that supports our Simple Life Plan. At the end of the chapter, I will share helpful tips that will help us stay on target with our finances and help us live our lives more simply.

Living within our means is one of the most important, if not the most important, thing we can do for our overall well-being and happiness. Using our financial resources unwisely and spending more than we can afford will cause dire consequences and affect our ability to stay focused on the important parts of our lives. When we live outside our means, our time, energy, and focus are dominated by money problems. To meet these financial needs, we may have to work more hours or take on additional jobs just to cover our expenses. We may have to borrow money and send ourselves deeper into debt, which may keep us awake at night making tough decisions about how we will ration money to our creditors.

Living outside of our means is dangerous. When money dominates our time and energy and becomes our focal point, we lose sight of the important things in our lives. When this happens, we place a wedge between us and all the things that give us happiness, which separates us from the very things that make life worth living. Living within our financial means is critical to keeping us on target with our Simple Life Plan and being happy—finding purpose in our lives and living the simple life.

Some of us falsely believe that if we were only rich, all of our problems would vanish. I assure you they won't. Money alone does not bring us happiness. The unrealistic wants in our lives fool us into believing that money solves all problems, but it doesn't. Happiness comes from focusing our money, time, and energy on the things that are most important to us. We must use our money to support our Simple Life Plan priorities—the most important things in our lives—before it can bring us true happiness.

Being the richest person in the world will not make us happy. I have been fortunate throughout my business career to be associated with many multimillionaires. I can tell you firsthand that their money has not made them happy. They go through the same trials and tribulations we do. They have to make tough decisions about money issues from time to time just like we do. The only difference between the financial decisions they make and ours is their decisions have more zeros. I think if you ask wealthy people if money makes them happy, they will tell you that having a lot of money has not made them happy. Money makes life more comfortable, allows them to do things they otherwise may not be able to do, and gives them more financial leeway in crisis situations, but money alone does not bring them happiness.

I will even go a step farther. If the population of the United States were spread evenly so that there were just as many poor people in the country as there were rich people, I can almost guarantee you that there would be more happy poor people than rich ones. Why? Because of poor people's lack of financial resources, they are forced to focus their spending on the most important things in their lives. They don't have the luxury of extra money to waste on unimportant things. Therefore, much of their money is spent on the things that mean the most to them.

Wealthy people, on the other hand, because of their money excesses, tend to forget what's important and more readily allow the influence of unrealistic wants that come with lots of money to enter into their lives. They allow the pursuit of money to draw their attention away from what's most important. Once people lose focus on the important things in their lives, unrealistic wants begin to control their decisions and moves them away from all the things that give life meaning and, instead, leads them down a path of unfulfilled dreams and goals. In the end, their lives lose direction and balance, which leads to unhappiness—that emptiness we sometimes feel.

Now don't get me wrong, not all wealthy people are this way. Some stay focused and keep the course, but many let the lure of unrealistic wants ruin their lives. Happiness is not determined by how much money we have, but is the result of how we use our money to stay close to the things that give our lives meaning. Happiness comes through focusing our financial means on the important people, activities, and things we identified with our priority lists.

Although money alone will not bring us happiness, I don't want us to think that having a lot of money will make us unhappy. Money is good when it is used correctly. Money gives us freedom from having to worry so much about unexpected expenses. When our car breaks down without warning, having money stashed away for emergencies reduces our stress level so we don't have to worry about where the money is going to come from to repair our car. It is nice to have extra money to take our significant others out for a nice meal and a movie. It is nice to have the money to go on a great vacation getaway with our families. Having extra money can be a great stress reliever. Money in itself is good. It is only when we let the influence of unrealistic wants into our lives and let the love of money control our decisions that money becomes a problem.

How do you spend your money? Do you have any idea how much money you spend on things from month to month? If you don't have a clue, don't be ashamed. Most of us don't. Most of us live from paycheck to paycheck and don't have any idea where our money really goes. If we have money left over at the end of the month, we think we have done well, but have we?

It's time to change our money-management strategy. It's time to start focusing on where every penny is spent. Is our money being used to further the life we want to live, or is it being used to support a life that takes us away from the important people and things in our lives? Remember, we are designing the life we want to live. Now it's time to take the next step of the process and design our financial strategy so that it focuses on the priorities in our lives.

To establish our Financial Means Plan, we must first determine where our money is going. A good place to start is our checking account and credit card statements. They give us a running history of what money we spent with a check, debit card, or credit card and provide an accurate resource for collecting information about our spending habits.

Collect six to twelve months of your checking account and credit card statements. Of course, the farther you go back, the more accurate your final analysis will be, but at a minimum use six to twelve months. In my particular case, I went back a full year. I wanted to make sure that I collected expenses on any periodic payments I might have overlooked that are not made on a monthly basis. An example would be a bill paid only once a year such as property taxes or a safe deposit box rental. Expenses collected beyond twelve months may not be relevant due to the age of the information.

In addition, we need to collect information on purchases we made with cash. This may take a little more effort to collect, but it is important that we collect this information. A dollar spent here and there adds up over time and can play a major role in our overall financial situation. The best way I have found to collect these expenses is by using my bank statements and creating a single expense item on my financial worksheet. The theory is, if we withdraw cash when making a deposit or purchase or by withdrawing money from an ATM, we count it as cash spent. We won't track what we spend it on, but once cash is withdrawn, it is considered spent. We assume it was spent on something important and necessary to our day-to-day living. I will go into more detail later in the example.

Finally, we must establish our income, both gross and net. Income information is collected last because, of the three types of information we are collecting, it is the easiest to collect. Using the same time period we used for expenses, we collect information on any money we were paid. Both gross and net income amounts must be collected because they are important in understanding what money we have to cover expenses.

What is gross and net income? Gross income is the money we make before taxes and deductions—usually the amount quoted to us as a person's salary or hourly rate. Our taxes are based on this amount. Net income is the amount of money we actually take home or put into the bank after taxes and deductions. This amount of money covers our day-to-day expenses. Both amounts are important, and I will go into more detail later.

Once we have collected our income and expense information, it is time to start organizing it. Take a sheet of paper or use Microsoft Excel® or any other worksheet software to organize everything. If you are familiar with Excel®, using this program will be best for organizing your financial information. It allows you to manipulate the data easily and illustrate where your money is going. If you don't have access to a worksheet program, maybe you know someone who does who would be willing to help you organize everything. Even if you have to use paper, start by listing your income and expenses for each month. For illustrative purposes, we will use our fictitious characters John and Kristina Pennywise to demonstrate the collection and organization of their financial data. Your financial information will be pulled together and organized the same way.

One word of caution; don't get hung up on the numbers presented in the examples. The illustrations presented through our fictitious characters John and Kristina Pennywise are just that—fictional. The numbers are all made up. The important thing to understand while going through this chapter is the process. The particular income and expense numbers presented are not important. What's important is that you understand the process so you can apply it to your financial goals—your simple life. With that being said, let's get started.

70-30 Financial System

Before we go any further, it's time to introduce you to the 70-30 Financial System. Just like the four priority lists we established in the previous chapter, we need a financial process to keep our spending on track to support our priorities. I call this plan the 70-30 Financial System. I developed this system several years ago, and it has always worked for me. This method is our road map to financial stability, and it will establish our Financial Means Plan. Most of all, this system will establish spending boundaries and keep our spending within our available resources. If you want to tweak this method or have another system that you would rather use, feel free to do so. Controlling our spending and freeing up resources to focus on our priorities are our main goals. Use whatever system best fits your needs.

So what does 70-30 mean? Quite simply, the 70-30 Financial System designates how we spend our income. The number 70 signifies that 70 percent of our gross income will be dedicated to our essential day-to-day living expenses. These are the things that are necessary—the stuff we can't live without. These expenses include things like housing, food, clothing, transportation, and the somewhat overlooked elephant in the room—taxes. Anything that we spend on our day-to-day living is included in this category. Our goal is to limit these expenses to 70 percent of our gross income.

The number 30 represents three important spending categories that go hand in hand with our daily living expenses. The first 10 percent is dedicated to things that are not necessarily essential to day-to-day living, but are important to us. Unlike our 70 percent category of things we can't live without, this category includes things that are nice to have but could be eliminated if necessary. Expenditures in this category are considered second-level needs. Some would argue that these expenditures are our luxury items or our wants above our needs. I'm not sure that assessment is totally accurate, but suffice it to say that if we get into a financial bind, these are the expenses we can live without if necessary. Our goal is to limit these expenses to 10 percent of our gross income.

The second 10 percent represents the income we are going to designate to short-term savings and long-term investing for the future. Half or 5 percent is dedicated to short-term savings designated for unanticipated expenses. The thought here is that we always want a stash of cash to protect us during unforeseen events. This percentage provides added comfort that when these unexpected things happen—and they will—we have resources to cover these expenses to keep us from digging a financial hole that may affect our priorities and get us off track. Our goal is to set aside 5 percent of our gross income to cover these types of expenses. This money is normally kept in cash stored in some type of savings account or other very liquid asset that can easily be converted to cash.

The other 5 percent of this category is used for long-term investing for our future. This money can be invested in a 401(k) or other retirement plan, investments such as stocks and bonds, planned upgrades to our home, investment property, appreciating assets, or any other expenditure that is used to enhance or secure our future. Our goal again is to spend 5 percent of our gross income preparing for the future. No matter how young we are or feel it is never too early or late to prepare for the future.

The final 10 percent represents the money we invest through charities and gifts to others. This category includes donations to our church, charitable organizations, and all the money we spend to help others. It is good to give a percentage of our income to others. It not only makes us feel better about ourselves, but donating money to a good cause makes the world around us a better place to live. Be especially careful to document any expenditure in this category that could be used as a tax deduction on income taxes at the end of the year. Our goal is to spend 10 percent of our gross income in this way.

Why is it so important to invest in others? In a 2008 study, British Columbia psychologists Elizabeth Dunn, Lara Aknin, and Michael Norton found that spending money on our bills and expenses did not have the same rewarding effect as spending money on others through donations to charities or gifts.[33] In their paper "Spending Money on Others Promotes Happiness," they concluded, through three different studies, that spending money on charities and others is much more fulfilling and gave more satisfaction to their participants than spending the money on themselves or bills. They went on to say that level of wealth and the size of the donation didn't matter. Spending as little as five dollars on someone else made a significant difference in a participant's happiness. Based on their conclusions, investing money in others and giving to charity are essential to being happy and should always be incorporated into our Financial Means Plan.

Based on the 70-30 Financial System, a person making $100,000 would assign $70,000 of their gross income to cover essential day-to-day living expenses. In addition, $30,000 would be divided into three $10,000 accounts and allocated to cover important but expendable expenses, short-term savings and long-term investments, and charities and gifts to others. This simple allocation of money establishes our financial goals and sets limits on our expenditures.

Why do we categorize our gross income this way? The 70-30 Financial System gives us a process of organizing our expenses and provides a measuring stick to evaluate our financial stewardship. In the end, staying on track financially and living within our means are vitally important to keeping us on course with our Simple Life Plan and gives us the means to live our lives more simply.

Now the 70-30 Financial System is not perfect. Life happens, and sometimes it doesn't take prisoners. There will be times in our lives when we will need to rob from Peter to pay Paul when something unforeseen happens that is beyond the reach of our short-term financial resources. However, the 70-30 Financial System—if we follow it—gives us the structure necessary to prepare for these times and the flexibility to meet these needs when life happens. By designating our gross income into predefined expense categories and sticking to the plan, the odds increase that the money will be there when we need it most. As we go through the illustrative example with John and Kristina, we will go into more detail about how the 70-30 Financial System keeps us focused on living within our means.

John and Kristina Pennywise's Financial Means Plan

John Pennywise works for a large company and lives in Louisville, Kentucky. John is married to his wife, Kristina, who also works for a large employer in the area.

John collected the past twelve months of their income and expenses. Gross income was determined by collecting a year's worth of pay stubs from both their jobs kept in a drawer in their kitchen. Each pay stub was carefully itemized and recorded by month to include gross income, taxes, and deductions. Figure 1 illustrates a summary of this work and shows John and Kristina's gross income and net income over the past twelve months. The full worksheets illustrating all of his work can be found at the Simple Life Publishing website (www.SimpleLifePublishing.com).

Since they usually pay their expenses by check, debit card, or credit card, they collected their monthly expenditures from their bank and credit card statements. John listed all expenditures by month to correspond with their income for each period.

Expenditures of cash were a little more difficult to capture. Neither John nor Kristina wanted to make the effort to track their purchases by

Figure 1

Name/Description	Income												
	Jan	Feb	Mar	Apr	May	Jun	Jul	Aug	Sep	Oct	Nov	Dec	Total
John's Gross Pay	3,687.12	2,887.27	3,267.18	3,287.12	3,287.12	3,880.47	3,287.12	3,880.47	3,287.12	3,287.12	3,880.47	3,287.12	41,205.70
John's Net Income	2,793.52	2,101.26	2,396.85	2,413.41	2,414.88	2,930.24	2,413.84	2,900.25	2,413.84	2,373.84	2,900.25	2,373.84	30,426.05
Kristina's Gross Pay	3,282.38	2,582.33	2,982.38	3,082.38	2,982.38	3,112.17	2,982.38	3,112.17	2,982.38	2,982.38	3,112.17	2,982.38	36,177.88
Kristina's Net Income	2,557.14	1,944.57	2,271.24	2,360.03	2,271.17	2,365.47	2,269.39	2,355.27	2,246.90	2,269.39	2,355.47	2,269.39	27,535.45
Total Gross Income	6,969.50	5,469.60	6,249.56	6,369.50	6,269.50	6,992.64	6,269.50	6,992.64	6,269.50	6,269.50	6,992.64	6,269.50	77,383.58
Total Net Income	5,350.67	4,045.83	4,668.09	4,773.45	4,686.06	5,295.71	4,683.24	5,255.52	4,660.75	4,643.24	5,255.72	4,643.24	57,961.50

cash over an extended period of time, so they decided to compare the deposit entries on their bank statements against their check stubs. When the two differed, they took the difference of the two and recorded it as a cash withdrawal. In addition, they added the cash that was withdrawn from a money machine or received as cash back through debit card purchases on each bank statement to this total. They recorded the cash withdrawn as a separate line item under the expense column of each month. In their Financial Means Plan, they assumed that, if they withdrew cash, it was spent on miscellaneous expenses not significant enough to warrant a distribution into a predefined category. However, it was still counted as an essential expense. Your bank should be able to help you collect this information if, for whatever reason, it is not readily available to you.

Although John and Kristina chose not to track their cash purchases over a period of time, tracking your cash is important if you spend an extraordinary amount of cash. Just remember, that the longer you track your cash purchases, the more accurate the information you collect will be. Try to find a happy medium between the length of time you track your purchases and the effort required to do so. Use whichever method makes more sense to you. However, the current trend seems to indicate that very few people use a significant amount of cash for purchases today because of the ease of using a debit or credit card.

One final thought before we jump deep into John and Kristina's finances. I need to talk briefly about reimbursable expenses. Some of us spend money on behalf of our employers that is reimbursable. Money spent while on a business trip, having lunch with a customer, or on office supplies are examples of this type of expense. Do not include reimbursed expenses in the calculation of your income and expenses. This type of expense has a net effect of zero on your finances and should not be included. It will only skew your results and make your gross income look larger than it really is. Count these expenses only if you are not reimbursed. If you want to track reimbursed business expenses for your own records, keep them separate from your other expenditures and put them under a heading of reimbursable expenses. That way, once you are reimbursed, the money you receive will offset the expense and will result in a zero effect on your finances. Remember, unreimbursed employer expenditures may also be tax deductible.

Once John collected all of Kristina's and his income and expenses, he created the worksheet shown in Figure 2. As you can see from the worksheet,

John and Kristina have a combined gross income of $77,383.58. After taxes and deductions withheld by their employers, they have a net income of $57,961.50 to spend anyway they see fit. Their total expenses, investments, and giving for this same period was $55,526.43. Please keep in mind that these numbers are fictional and serve only as a reference to explain the process.

A quick review of the worksheet shows a problem. Although their total yearly income covered their total expenses by $2,435.07, in four of the past twelve months, they spent more than they earned. Although most of us would like this not to happen, because of periodic payments throughout the year that are above and beyond our normal monthly expenses, it sometimes happens to the most careful of us. I suspect the difference between their income and expenses in these months was carried with a credit card balance or the money was pulled from their savings. As John and Kristina look at their income and expenses through the 70-30 Financial System, they will better understand their shortfalls and plan ways to save money for these times or reduce their expenses during these months to bring these numbers back into line. If they don't take action but keep going down this path, with an unexpected expense, their finances could quickly spiral out of control.

Remember, the overriding goal of our Financial Means Plan is to live within our means, within our available resources. If expenses exceed income, we will fall short of our goal and undoubtedly experience added stress and an unnecessary burden in our lives. Living within our means is vital to living a simple life.

Analyzing John and Kristina's Financial Information

To address the expense overage and to apply income and expenses to the 70-30 Financial System, let's start organizing John and Kristina's expenses into the four main categories of the plan and see how they are really doing. Remember the four categories are essential day-to-day living expenses, important but not necessarily essential expenses, short-term savings and long-term investments, and charities and gifts to others. Using the 70-30 Financial System formula and John and Kristina's financial information, the four categories break down their gross income the following way:

Figure 2

Name/Description	Jan	Feb	Mar	Apr	May	Jun	Jul	Aug	Sep	Oct	Nov	Dec	Total
Income													
John's Gross Pay	3,687.12	2,887.27	3,267.18	3,287.12	3,287.12	3,880.47	3,287.12	3,880.47	3,287.12	3,287.12	3,880.47	3,287.12	41,205.70
John's Net Income	2,793.52	2,101.26	2,396.85	2,413.41	2,414.88	2,930.24	2,413.84	2,900.25	2,413.84	2,373.84	2,900.25	2,373.84	30,426.05
Kristina's Gross Pay	3,282.38	2,582.33	2,982.38	3,082.38	2,982.38	3,112.17	2,982.38	3,112.17	2,982.38	2,982.38	3,112.17	2,982.38	36,177.88
Kristina's Net Income	2,557.14	1,944.57	2,271.24	2,360.03	2,271.17	2,365.47	2,269.39	2,355.27	2,246.90	2,269.39	2,355.47	2,269.39	27,535.45
Total Gross Income	6,969.50	5,469.60	6,249.56	6,369.50	6,269.50	6,992.64	6,269.50	6,992.64	6,269.50	6,269.50	6,992.64	6,269.50	77,383.58
Total Net Income	5,350.67	4,045.83	4,668.09	4,773.45	4,686.06	5,295.71	4,683.24	5,255.52	4,660.75	4,643.24	5,255.72	4,643.24	57,961.50
Expenses													
Total Expenses	4,293.16	3,703.54	4,882.27	5,022.04	4,143.17	5,192.77	4,413.98	3,970.58	3,723.78	3,916.78	6,320.42	5,943.94	55,526.43
Total Net Inc - Exp	1,057.51	342.29	(214.18)	(248.59)	542.89	102.94	269.26	1,284.94	936.97	726.46	(1,064.70)	(1,300.70)	2,435.07

Essential Expenses (70%) $54,168.50
Nonessential Expenses (10%) $7,738.36
Short-Term Savings and Long-Term Investments (10%)
    Short-Term Savings (5%) $3,869.18
    Long-Term Investments (5%) $3,869.18
Charities and Gifts to Others (10%) $7,738.36

The worksheet in Figure 3 summarizes John and Kristina's work, assigning their financial information into these categories.

Based on the 70-30 Financial System, John and Kristina have some work to do. Figure 2 shows that four out of twelve months their expenses exceeded their income. Although they ended the year with a positive balance, more than likely they had to use savings or carry a credit card balance to weather the storm. Figure 3 helps us to identify the problem, showing John and Kristina's financial information broken into the four 70-30 categories.

The first problem identified is the essential day-to-day expenses exceed their 70 percent goal by $2,644.20. John and Kristina must make some tough decisions to bring these expenses back into line.

The second problem identified concerns the important but nonessential expenses. Just like the essential day-to-day expenses, they exceed the 10 percent goal by $758.88. Although the overage is less than it was with the essential expenses, the challenge to reduce these expenses below the goal of 10 percent is still just as real. The difference with this category is that John and Kristina have already identified these expenses as expendable, if necessary. In the months in which their expenses are greater than their income, John and Kristina have agreed to watch their spending more carefully in their nonessential category to help offset this shortfall. Nonetheless, they must immediately reduce expenses in this category by at least the $758.88 or more if they decide to move some of their essential expenses into the nonessential category to protect them from being eliminated.

The third problem identified is John and Kristina's short-term savings and long-term investments are underfunded. On their current pace, the funds will never support the simple life they are trying to build or keep them focused on their identified priorities. To bring their short-term savings into line, John and Kristina need to fund this account by another $2,969.18 per year. Likewise, the long-term investments need to be funded

LIVE THE SIMPLE LIFE YOU DREAM ABOUT

Figure 3

Income

Name/Description	Jan	Feb	Mar	Apr	May	Jun	Jul	Aug	Sep	Oct	Nov	Dec	Total
John's Gross Pay	3,687.12	2,887.27	3,267.18	3,287.12	3,287.12	3,880.47	3,287.12	3,880.47	3,287.12	3,287.12	3,880.47	3,287.12	41,205.70
Kristina's Gross Pay	3,282.38	2,582.33	2,982.38	3,082.38	2,982.38	3,112.17	2,982.38	3,112.17	2,982.38	2,982.38	3,112.17	2,982.38	36,177.88
Total	6,969.50	5,469.60	6,249.56	6,369.50	6,269.50	6,992.64	6,269.50	6,992.64	6,269.50	6,269.50	6,992.64	6,269.50	77,383.58

Expenses

Essential Day-to-Day Expenses ($54,168.50)

Name/Description	Jan	Feb	Mar	Apr	May	Jun	Jul	Aug	Sep	Oct	Nov	Dec	Total
Total Ess Expenses	4,421.48	4,007.52	5,377.64	5,272.09	4,142.75	4,272.17	4,376.74	4,327.00	4,328.12	4,311.75	6,108.99	5,866.46	56,812.70
												Diff	(2,644.20)
												Net	57.99

Important But Not Essential Expenses ($7,738.36)

	Jan	Feb	Mar	Apr	May	Jun	Jul	Aug	Sep	Oct	Nov	Dec	Total
Total NonEss Expenses	544.56	476.83	365.94	672.05	862.91	1,653.94	902.55	482.11	283.46	560.34	999.76	692.79	8,497.24
												Diff	(758.88)
												Net	526.28

Short Term Savings & Long Term Investments ($7,738.36)

Short Term Savings ($3,869.18)

	Jan	Feb	Mar	Apr	May	Jun	Jul	Aug	Sep	Oct	Nov	Dec	Total
Total	100.00	50.00	100.00	50.00	100.00	50.00	100.00	50.00	100.00	50.00	100.00	50.00	900.00
												Diff	2,969.18

Long Term Investments ($3,869.18)

	Jan	Feb	Mar	Apr	May	Jun	Jul	Aug	Sep	Oct	Nov	Dec	Total
Total	245.96	192.96	220.16	223.96	220.96	248.58	220.96	248.58	220.96	220.96	248.58	220.96	2,733.56
												Diff	1,135.62

Charities & Gifts To Others ($7,738.36)

	Jan	Feb	Mar	Apr	May	Jun	Jul	Aug	Sep	Oct	Nov	Dec	Total
Total	600.00	400.00	400.00	400.00	400.00	665.00	400.00	600.00	400.00	400.00	600.00	740.00	6,005.00
												Diff	1,733.36

by another $1,135.62. Where will the funding come from? They will fund these accounts by reducing the essential and nonessential expenses to levels below their stated goals of 70 percent and 10 percent respectively. Without these cost reductions, the plan falls apart, and they will never fully achieve the financial goals of their Simple Life Plan.

The final problem illustrated in Figure 3 is the money designated for charities and gifts to others is also underfunded. To bring this spending goal to its 10 percent level, John and Kristina must increase funding of this expense category by $1,733.36 a year. Remember, as studies show, money spent here, more than anywhere else, gives us the most satisfaction and brings happiness to our lives.

John and Kristina's Solution to Meet Their Financial Goals

After much thought and analysis, John and Kristina decided on the following plan of action to bring their finances in line with the 70-30 Financial System allocations. The worksheet in Figure 4 is their proposed solution.

Every line item highlighted on the worksheet is being eliminated. Under the essential day-to-day expenses, John and Kristina decided that they no longer needed their landline phone service in addition to the unlimited cell phone plan they have in place. Several of their friends dropped their home phones several months ago and have assured them they will not miss it. John and Kristina have decided to take their friends' advice and eliminate this monthly cost.

Three other subscription services are also being canceled. John and Kristina decided they rarely have time to watch their online movie channel anymore and could reduce the cost of their cable subscription. They also rarely use their satellite radio service and agreed they could go back to listening to local radio stations and CDs. The final subscription eliminated is the monthly bank fraud-detection service. Although eliminating this service may add some additional risk to their credit card purchases, they feel the cost of the service outweighs the risk. In addition, they consider this risk even lower since they have vowed to reduce their credit card purchases in the future.

In addition to reducing their credit card purchases, they agreed to withdraw cash from their savings account to pay off their credit card balance and

Figure 4

Income

Name/Description	Jan	Feb	Mar	Apr	May	Jun	Jul	Aug	Sep	Oct	Nov	Dec	Total
John's Gross Pay	3,687.12	2,887.27	3,267.18	3,287.12	3,287.12	3,880.47	3,287.12	3,880.47	3,287.12	3,287.12	3,880.47	3,287.12	41,205.70
Kristina's Gross Pay	3,282.38	2,582.33	2,982.38	3,082.38	2,982.38	3,112.17	2,982.38	3,112.17	2,982.38	2,982.38	3,112.17	2,982.38	36,177.88
Total	6,969.50	5,469.60	6,249.56	6,369.50	6,269.50	6,992.64	6,269.50	6,992.64	6,269.50	6,269.50	6,992.64	6,269.50	77,383.58

Expenses

Essential Day-to-Day Expenses ($54,168.50)

Name/Description	Jan	Feb	Mar	Apr	May	Jun	Jul	Aug	Sep	Oct	Nov	Dec	Total
Land Line Phone Service	52.77	60.27	53.73	53.73	53.73	53.73	53.73	60.88	53.73	53.73	53.73	72.22	675.98
Movie Service	10.59	10.59	10.59	10.59	10.59	10.59	10.59	10.59	10.59	10.59	8.09	8.09	122.08
Yard Service	64.00				160.00		288.00	128.00	96.00		192.00		928.00
Satellite Radio			166.35	113.90									280.25
Credit Card Payment	50.00	50.00	50.00	50.00	50.00	50.00	50.00	50.00	50.00	50.00	50.00	50.00	600.00
Bank Fraud Det	7.99	7.99	7.99	7.99	7.99	7.99	7.99	7.99	7.99	7.99	7.99	7.99	95.88
Total Ess Expenses	4,421.48	4,007.52	5,377.64	5,272.09	4,142.75	4,272.17	4,376.74	4,327.00	4,328.12	4,311.75	6,108.99	5,866.46	56,812.70
												Diff	(2,644.20)
												Net	57.99

Important But Not Essential Expenses ($7,738.36)

Name/Description	Jan	Feb	Mar	Apr	May	Jun	Jul	Aug	Sep	Oct	Nov	Dec	Total
Popular Mechanics				16.93									16.93
Timbercreek Rentals						439.56	439.55						879.11
Doublehead Resort								120.00		269.12			389.12
Total NonEss Expenses	544.56	476.83	365.94	672.05	862.91	1,653.94	902.55	482.11	283.46	560.34	999.76	692.79	8,497.24
												Diff	(758.88)
												Net	526.28

Short Term Savings & Long Term Investments ($7,738.36)

Short Term Savings ($3,869.18)

	Jan	Feb	Mar	Apr	May	Jun	Jul	Aug	Sep	Oct	Nov	Dec	Total
Total	100.00	50.00	100.00	50.00	100.00	50.00	100.00	50.00	100.00	50.00	100.00	50.00	900.00
												Diff	2,969.18

Long Term Investments ($3,869.18)

	Jan	Feb	Mar	Apr	May	Jun	Jul	Aug	Sep	Oct	Nov	Dec	Total
Total	245.96	192.96	220.16	223.96	220.96	248.58	220.96	248.58	220.96	220.96	248.58	220.96	2,733.56
												Diff	1,135.62

Charities & Gifts To Others ($7,738.36)

	Jan	Feb	Mar	Apr	May	Jun	Jul	Aug	Sep	Oct	Nov	Dec	Total
Total	600.00	400.00	400.00	400.00	400.00	665.00	400.00	600.00	400.00	400.00	600.00	740.00	6,005.00
												Diff	1,733.36

eliminate this monthly payment. This move alone will wipe out $600 a year from their expenses and eliminate future interest payments. We will discuss the use of credit cards later in the financial tips section.

The last item to be eliminated from the essential day-to-day expenses is the yard service. John has agreed to pull out the lawn mower, dust it off, and take up this task again. John and Kristina agree that John needs more exercise to improve his health. Doing yard work will be a great way to get some of the exercise he needs and save money at the same time. Who knows, by getting a little exercise, John may also help reduce the couple's long-term medical expenses.

Eliminating these line items from the essential expenses has reduced their yearly expenditures in this category by $2,702.19 and brought it under the 70 percent goal by $57.99. Granted, John and Kristina could have moved some of these expenses to the important but nonessential expense category to bring it under budget, but they decided not to pass the buck and cut their losses on expenses they felt they could live without.

John and Kristina followed the same process with their important but nonessential expense category. They canceled a magazine subscription and put on hold two mini-vacations they have taken over the past several years until they are in a better financial position. They still have one vacation they look forward to each year. These cost reductions meet their immediate need to reduce this category by $758.88 and save John and Kristina almost $1300 a year to bring this expense category under budget by $526.28.

In the months their expenses are greater than their income, they have agreed to watch their spending even more closely. They will reduce it wherever possible in the nonessential category and try to avoid carrying a credit card balance. If their expenses exceed their income in any month, they will use their short-term savings to cover any shortfalls. In addition, they will try to move some of their periodic payments to lighter outflow months to help balance their expenses throughout the year.

Now that John and Kristina have reduced their expenditures in their essential day-to-day and important but nonessential expense categories, they can take the money they saved here and invest it in themselves and others. From the analysis John and Kristina performed, they realized they were underfunding their short-term savings and long-term investments. To resolve their short-term savings shortfall, they are increasing their monthly deposits to their savings and credit union accounts by $2,940, spread throughout the year. This change will give John and Kristina $3,840 per year to meet unanticipated expenses and to meet shortfalls when they happen, which will keep them from having to use a credit card in all but emergency situations. If at the end of the year there is a balance in this account, they will shift some of this money into a more long-term savings account for future purchases or investments.

Likewise, the long-term investment accounts are being increased by $1,133.84. John and Kristina are increasing their contributions to John's 401(k) and Kristina's monthly annuity, and they are establishing a long-term savings account that will provide $360 per year to invest in other long-term investments such as stocks, bonds, or appreciating assets. The savings account is not much right now, but over time it will provide a good source of investment income as their salaries increase from year to year.

For the first time in John and Kristina's lives, they are setting aside money to invest in themselves. But it is not enough just to invest money in themselves. It is also vitally important to invest in others. In their charities and gifts to others account, they are increasing their giving by $1,730. Most of this increase is going to John and Kristina's church, and the rest is being consolidated through three account line items.

Figure 5 shows the results of John and Kristina's effort using the 70-30 Financial System. The resulting worksheet now becomes the preliminary budget for their Simple Life Plan. Their Financial Means Plan has been established, and it will serve them well if they stick to their 70-30 budget goals. Most of all, the 70-30 Financial System will allow them to focus on their priorities, invest in themselves and others, and live the simple life they dream about.

Shifting Financial Resources to Priorities

Now that John and Kristina have brought their spending back in line using the 70-30 Financial System and are living within their financial means, how do they refocus their spending on their priorities identified in their Simple Life Plan? Reviewing the priorities they identified, many of them, such as volunteering at the church, do not have a financial resource requirement. These priorities are more dependent on time resources than money requirements. However, several of the other priorities they identified, such as John's desire to attain an MBA or Kristina's priority to travel to Rome, will require monetary resources.

Figure 5

Name/Description	Jan	Feb	Mar	Apr	May	Jun	Jul	Aug	Sep	Oct	Nov	Dec	Total
Income													
John's Gross Pay	3,687.12	2,887.27	3,267.18	3,287.12	3,287.12	3,880.47	3,287.12	3,880.47	3,287.12	3,287.12	3,880.47	3,287.12	41,205.70
Kristina's Gross Pay	3,282.38	2,582.33	2,982.38	3,082.38	2,982.38	3,112.17	2,982.38	3,112.17	2,982.38	2,982.38	3,112.17	2,982.38	36,177.88
Total	6,969.50	5,469.60	6,249.56	6,369.50	6,269.50	6,992.64	6,269.50	6,992.64	6,269.50	6,269.50	6,992.64	6,269.50	77,383.58
Expenses													
Name/Description	Jan	Feb	Mar	Apr	May	Jun	Jul	Aug	Sep	Oct	Nov	Dec	Total
Essential Day-to-Day Expenses ($54,168.50)													
Total Ess Expenses	4,236.13	3,878.67	5,088.98	5,035.88	3,860.44	4,149.86	3,966.43	4,069.54	4,109.81	4,189.44	5,797.18	5,728.16	54,110.51
												Diff	57.99
Important But Not Essential Expenses ($7,738.36)													
Total NonEss Expenses	644.00	644.00	644.00	644.00	644.00	644.00	644.00	644.00	644.00	644.00	644.00	644.00	7,728.00
												Diff	10.36
Short Term Savings & Long Term Investments ($7,738.36)													
Short Term Savings ($3,869.18)													
Total	320.00	320.00	320.00	320.00	320.00	320.00	320.00	320.00	320.00	320.00	320.00	320.00	3,840.00
												Diff	29.18
Long Term Investments ($3,869.18)													
Total	345.65	277.66	312.65	317.65	313.65	348.51	313.65	348.51	313.65	313.65	348.51	313.65	3,867.40
												Diff	1.78
Charities & Gifts To Others ($7,738.36)													
Total	625.00	625.00	625.00	625.00	625.00	840.00	625.00	625.00	625.00	625.00	625.00	645.00	7,735.00
												Diff	3.36

What steps must John and Kristina take to start using their financial resources to fulfill the priorities in their lives and still live within their means? There are four steps. First, they must identify all the priorities within their lists that require financial resources. Second, they must determine the financial resources required and rank the priorities they identified based on cost and/or importance. Third, they must determine where monies in their Financial Means Plan can be reallocated, and fourth, they must commit the money they free up and use it to focus on their priorities in life. Let's look at each step in the process in more detail.

Step one requires John and Kristina to identify their priorities that call for financial resources. Looking back through their priority lists, they identified their top seven priorities that will require monetary resources:

John

- Get an MBA
- Learn to Scuba Dive
- Change Jobs
- Go to the NCAA Basketball Tourney
- Take My Dad to a NASCAR Race
- Clean the Furnace Each Year
- Lose Weight

Kristina

- Learn to Play the Guitar
- Go to Rome
- Learn to Scuba Dive
- Change My Hair Color & Style
- Write a Cookbook
- Hire Someone to Clean the House
- Lose Weight

Although there are several other priorities in the Things That Make Me Happy List that could from time to time require financial resources, John and Kristina agreed to stay within the suggested span of control and listed only their top seven priorities.

Step two requires John and Kristina to determine the financial resources required for each priority and rank them based on the cost and/or importance of the priority. Their current lists with estimated costs are shown below:

John

- Get an MBA ($80,000 to $100,000)
- Learn to Scuba Dive ($300)
- Change Jobs (Less than $100)
- Go to the NCAA Basketball Tourney ($1,500 to $1,700)
- Take My Dad to a NASCAR Race ($350)
- Clean the Furnace Each Year ($115)
- Lose Weight ($25 per month)

Kristina

- Learn to Play the Guitar ($35 per month)
- Go to Rome ($8,500)
- Learn to Scuba Dive ($300)
- Change My Hair Color & Style ($115)
- Write a Cookbook (Less than $50)
- Hire Someone to Clean the House ($125 per month)
- Lose Weight ($25 per month)

Now that we have identified the costs associated with each item on their lists, it is time to organize them by setting priorities. There are many ways to do this. I suggest you use the Low-Hanging Fruit, One-Time Fee, and Reoccurring Payment methods.

One rule of thought is to identify the "Low-Hanging Fruit." These are things that don't cost a lot of money to do that will give you immediate satisfaction with little or no investment. In John's case, his priority about changing jobs fits into this category. He estimates it will cost him less than

$100 dollars to get his resume ready and begin applying for jobs. A one-time expense of up to $100 will bring John immediate satisfaction that he is doing something positive to change his job situation. Kristina's "Low-Hanging Fruit" is her priority to write a cookbook. For less than $50, she can do the things necessary to begin her writing career. Taking this organizational approach, John and Kristina should put these two priorities on top of their "to do" list.

The second approach organizes their priorities based on a one-time fee. Examples of this type of expense are learning to scuba dive, going to the NCAA Basketball Tourney, a NASCAR race, and to Rome. Typically, you would organize these priorities based on importance and set aside money to accomplish these goals at some point in the future. If time is of the essence, you could also possibly charge the cost of these priorities to a credit card, as long as you pay it off at the end of the month when the charges come due. If the cost of the priority is above your ability to pay off when the credit card bill arrives, you should instead plan to set aside money and postpone tackling the priority until you can avoid paying interest.

The final approach to organize John and Kristina's priorities is based on reoccurring costs associated with a monthly or periodic payment. John's MBA, cleaning the furnace, and losing weight all fall within this type of cost. For Kristina, learning to play guitar, changing her hair color, losing weight, and hiring someone to clean their home meet the reoccurring cost definition. These costs usually require an offsetting reduction in spending somewhere else in the budget or, like John's MBA, a financial loan. These priorities require a regular payment they must budget for. Their priority lists, organized by the Low-Hanging Fruit, One-Time Fee, and Reoccurring Payment methods, are illustrated below:

John

- **Low-Hanging Fruit**
    - Change Jobs (Less than $100)

- **One-Time Fee**

- o Learn to Scuba Dive ($300)
- o Take My Dad to a NASCAR Race ($350)
- o Go to the NCAA Basketball Tourney ($1,500 to $1,700)

- **Reoccurring Payment**
  - o Lose Weight ($25 per month)
  - o Clean the Furnace Each Year ($115)
  - o Get an MBA ($80,000 to $100,000)

Kristina

- **Low-Hanging Fruit**
  - o Write a Cookbook (Less than $50)

- **One-Time Fee**
  - o Learn to Scuba Dive ($300)
  - o Go to Rome ($8,500)

- **Reoccurring Payment**
  - o Lose Weight ($25 per month)
  - o Learn to Play the Guitar ($35 per month)
  - o Change My Hair Color & Style ($115)
  - o Hire Someone to Clean the House ($125 per month)

Now that John and Kristina have established a cost for each priority and organized those that have a financial requirement, how do they find the money in their budget to accomplish their priorities? That brings us to step three: identifying money in our Financial Means Plan we can reallocate. Just like John and Kristina did when they analyzed their budget with the 70-30 Financial System and brought their spending back within their financial means, they must once again look at their budget and make some tough choices about how they spend their financial resources.

Through a detailed analysis of their spending, they can now make tough decisions about how they spend their money. Are the things they spend their money on necessary? Do they spend their monetary resources in ways that help them reach their life goals? Are their identified priorities important enough to change their spending habits to achieve their Simple Life Plan? These are the questions they must answer.

Just as with John and Kristina's budget, every line item of our budget must be open to the reallocation of funds to allow us to find the money we need to address our priorities in life. We must carefully review each place we spend money. We must reduce our spending wherever possible to free up financial resources we can use to focus on our priorities in our Simple Life Plan. If we don't make these difficult choices about our finances, we may never live our lives focusing on our priorities. And if we don't focus on our priorities, we will never be as happy as we could be. Our lives will be filled with regret that will keep us from the happiness waiting for us through the priorities we've identified.

So what did John and Kristina do? They went through their budget again and evaluated every line item, making sure it was contributing to living their lives according to their priorities. If an expense was determined not to be contributing to their priorities, it was marked for reallocation. The following expenditures were identified for reallocation:

Expenditures Available for Reallocation

- Cable TV
- Home Mortgage Refinance
- Home & Car Insurance

As you recall, John stated that he watched too much TV on his Things I Know I Should Be Doing Priority List. Although Kristina did not list it as a priority in any of her lists, she agreed that she watched too much TV as well. Because of their mutual agreement that they needed to reallocate financial resources to more important priorities, they decided to cancel their cable TV subscription and use a digital antenna to watch their favorite shows through their local stations. This action freed up over $1,800 per year that can now be used somewhere else.

Refinancing their home mortgage is another place John and Kristina chose to save money. The interest rates have been falling over the past several years so they contacted their mortgage lender to discuss refinancing their home. Through their discussions, they were able to lower their monthly payment by $188.66. This action produced a net yearly savings of $2,263.92, which they can shift to other more focused priorities.

Finally, John and Kristina have been meaning to shop around for insurance on their home and automobiles, but they kept putting it off. It had been several years since they have reviewed their insurance, and they felt like they were paying too much. After collecting several quotes, they were able to reduce their car insurance costs by $421.23 per year and their home insurance by $247, for a total yearly savings of $668.23. All the cost savings together added up to over $4,700 per year. If you include the savings they found during their earlier review when they brought their spending back within their financial means, John and Kristina found over $4,800 they can reallocate to more important priorities. See Figure 6 for the recap.

How should John and Kristina spend their newly found money on their priorities? This is decided in step four of the process as they allocate the monies they freed up to their priorities. As for their Low-Hanging Fruit, they are going to start working on these priorities immediately. Since the estimated costs are so low, they have agreed to pay for any expenses related to these priorities out of their pocket as they are incurred.

One-Time Fee priorities, except for the NASCAR race and trip to Rome, will be paid for out of their newly reallocated funds as they are realized and redirected to their short-term savings. These funds will allow John and Kristina to take scuba diving lessons together and meet their priority of spending more time with each other. In addition, the reallocation will allow John to attend next year's NCAA Basketball Tournament, something he has dreamed about for a long time. The cost to accomplish these priorities equals $2,300 and leaves a balance of over $2,500 in the reallocated fund money. The NASCAR race will be paid for with the Charities and Gifts to Others Account since it is a gift to John's dad. Monies within that account will be adjusted to cover the cost. Finally, the trip to Rome is being postponed for now. Monies for this trip will be collected by allocating any savings realized throughout the year to short-term savings when actual spending is less than what was budgeted. Both John and Kristina feel that this approach will help them get to Rome sooner by motivating them to find additional money that can be reallocated from less important priorities.

LIVE THE SIMPLE LIFE YOU DREAM ABOUT

Figure 6

Income

Name/Description	Jan	Feb	Mar	Apr	May	Jun	Jul	Aug	Sep	Oct	Nov	Dec	Total
John's Gross Pay	3,687.12	2,887.27	3,267.18	3,287.12	3,287.12	3,880.47	3,287.12	3,880.47	3,287.12	3,287.12	3,880.47	3,287.12	41,205.70
Kristina's Gross Pay	3,282.38	2,582.33	2,982.38	3,082.38	2,982.38	3,112.17	2,982.38	3,112.17	2,982.38	2,982.38	3,112.17	2,982.38	36,177.88
Total	6,969.50	5,469.60	6,249.56	6,369.50	6,269.50	6,992.64	6,269.50	6,992.64	6,269.50	6,269.50	6,992.64	6,269.50	77,383.58

Expenses

Essential Day-to-Day Expenses ($54,168.50)

Name/Description	Jan	Feb	Mar	Apr	May	Jun	Jul	Aug	Sep	Oct	Nov	Dec	Total
Mortgage Co	867.12	867.12	867.12	867.12	867.12	867.12	867.12	867.12	867.12	867.12	867.12	867.12	10,405.44
Home Insurance				837.87									837.87
Cable Co	0.00	0.00	0.00	0.00	0.00	0.00	0.00	0.00	0.00	0.00	0.00	0.00	0.00
Car Insurance			940.12								940.12		1,880.24
Total Ess Expenses	3,900.78	3,537.47	4,560.78	4,447.68	3,519.24	3,808.66	3,625.23	3,728.34	3,768.61	3,848.24	5,221.75	5,386.96	49,353.73
												Diff	4,814.77

Important But Not Essential Expenses ($7,738.36)

	Jan	Feb	Mar	Apr	May	Jun	Jul	Aug	Sep	Oct	Nov	Dec	Total
Total NonEss Expenses	644.00	644.00	644.00	644.00	644.00	644.00	644.00	644.00	644.00	644.00	644.00	644.00	7,728.00
												Diff	10.36

Short Term Savings & Long Term Investments ($7,738.36)

	Jan	Feb	Mar	Apr	May	Jun	Jul	Aug	Sep	Oct	Nov	Dec	Total
Short Term Savings ($3,869.18)													
Total	320.00	320.00	320.00	320.00	320.00	320.00	320.00	320.00	320.00	320.00	320.00	320.00	3,840.00
												Diff	29.18
Long Term Investments ($3,869.18)													
Total	345.65	277.66	312.65	317.65	313.65	348.51	313.65	348.51	313.65	313.65	348.51	313.65	3,867.40
												Diff	1.78

Charities & Gifts To Others ($7,738.36)

	Jan	Feb	Mar	Apr	May	Jun	Jul	Aug	Sep	Oct	Nov	Dec	Total
Total	625.00	625.00	625.00	625.00	625.00	840.00	625.00	625.00	625.00	625.00	625.00	645.00	7,735.00
												Diff	3.36

The Reoccurring Payment priorities, like the One-Time Fee priorities will be paid out of the reallocated funds they found. Cleaning the furnace yearly, learning to play the guitar, and hiring someone to clean their house will all be paid out of this money. Changing Kristina's hair color and style can be paid for with monies that are currently budgeted and will not require any additional money from the reallocated funds. However, John's MBA priority has been put on hold for now. He hopes to find a new employer during his job search that will assist him with this priority through tuition reimbursement. Finally, John and Kristina are going to try to lose weight without using a paid weight-loss program. They both feel confident they know what needs to be done and have committed to encouraging each other to stay on track. Additionally, this gives them another activity they can do with each other to meet their priority to spend more time together. Total funds needed to meet these priorities equal $2,035 per year. That leaves a balance in the reallocated fund money of over $460. The $460 can now be allocated to the Rome trip savings fund, putting Kristina a step closer to her dream vacation.

The four-step process that John and Kristina used to find money to reallocate to their priorities will work for you too. To be honest, once we identify our priorities—the people, activities, and things—that are most important to us, it's fairly straightforward. Less important things we spend money on will jump off the page at us as we focus on our expenditures and how they support our priorities.

For some of us, this is the first time we have ever put our income and expenses on paper and seriously looked at our finances. Taking the time to go through this process forces us to make choices about how we spend our money. That's a good thing! We need to look at how we're spending our money from time to time to determine whether we are spending it in a way that is meeting our life's goals. If it's not, we need to adjust our spending to bring it in line with our priorities.

Once you have established your Financial Means Plan like John and Kristina have done, you need to look at your budget every year. Yearly is better than every three to five years because finances and priorities change over time, and you want to make sure you adjust your spending as quickly as you can to stay on target. Living within your means is essential to living a simpler life. The 70-30 Financial System, if you use the tool, will not only help keep you living within your means, it will keep your finances focused on your priorities. I hope you will use the process we just discussed to help you stay focused on living the simple life you dream about.

Sticking to Your Financial Means Plan

Now that our Financial Means Plan, or budget, has been established, how do we stick to it? There are many good books on the market about stretching your dollar and investing. In addition, financial advisors in your community are willing to sit down with you and discuss your priorities and goals and help you develop an investing strategy that fits your needs. I encourage you to seek out advice from these individuals. Their counsel will be invaluable to your success.

The following pages contain seven general tips that have been invaluable to me over the years that will help you stay focused on how you spend your money.

1. Think Through Every Purchase

Before every purchase, you should ask yourself several questions. Can I afford this, and will it allow me to stay on budget? Will this purchase help me meet my financial goals and priorities? How much is enough? Do I have room in my life for this item, or will it just further clutter it? I'm sure there are many more questions we can come up with, but the main thought here is that before we make a purchase, we should make sure we really need what we are about to spend money on.

Never buy something you really don't need. Also, never buy more than you need. Having stuff sitting around collecting dust only clutters your living and adds stress to your life. Can I do without it? What value does this purchase bring to my life? Will this purchase provide happiness and give me more pleasure than I already have? If you have trouble answering any of these questions, maybe you should reconsider spending the money.

2. Reduce Credit Card Purchases

A credit card should never carry a balance from month to month. It is okay to use credit cards, but we should never purchase more than we can pay off at the end of the month. Unlike some people think, a credit card is not to be used as a source of income, but as a vehicle to track purchases, reduce the cash we carry, or provide quick money in an emergency. When we use it, we should never buy more than we can pay off at the end of the month. We want to avoid paying interest on purchases at all cost.

If possible, we should use a credit card that gives us cash back on purchases. One, two, three, or even five percent returned to our account doesn't sound like much, but over time, it adds up and gives us a little relief from ever-increasing prices.

3. Buying on Credit

Purchase only large, high-priced ticket items such as a house or car on credit. In addition, you must be sure that you run the numbers and make certain that the monthly commitment you are making falls comfortably within your Financial Means Plan. You may also want to run an amortization schedule to look at how much the credit is costing you. If you save for a future purchase as part of your savings plan, you may be able to buy some large ticket items such as appliances and, yes, even a new car with money from savings and avoid the cost of credit. The cost of credit is expensive, and we should avoid it whenever possible by using a zero-interest credit arrangement or through using cash from our long-term savings account.

4. Avoid Impulse Buying

When I was a kid, I used a trick that served me well. I grew up about six blocks from a mall. In the summertime, my friends and I would ride our bikes to the mall several times a week and spend the day looking through the stores. At first, I kept a pocketful of money, earned from my summer jobs, available to be ready to buy things that caught my eye while I was there. There was hardly a day that went by that I didn't come home with something that I bought—not expensive things, but things that called my name as I looked at them and as they burned a hole in the pocket holding my money.

The funny thing is that I stayed broke all the time, and I didn't really have anything to show for it. To earn additional money, I took on more projects in the neighborhood that took time away from being with my friends.

What did I do? I decided to stop my impulse buying by taking only enough money with me to buy a soda to quench my thirst on a hot day. If I found something I wanted to buy while I was at the mall, I forced myself to ride my bike all the way home to collect the money I needed. Once the money was in hand, I then had to peddle my bike all the way back to the mall to purchase it. You know what happened? I rarely ever went back to the mall to purchase something I thought I had to have while I was standing in front of it. The hot and humid Alabama climate was a natural motivator that kept me from returning to the mall and spending my hard-earned money.

Now I realize that carrying only enough money in our pockets to purchase a soda is not practical for an adult. What worked for a kid would never work for an adult, right?

When you are out shopping and something is calling your name and your money is burning a hole in your pocket, you should hide your money in another pocket and leave it there. Before you go shopping, you should make a list and stick to it! If you see something that you think you want buy while shopping for the items on your list, give yourself a twenty-four-hour reevaluation period before you purchase it. If in twenty-four hours you still want to purchase the shiny object that caught your eye, go ahead and purchase the item, as long as your budget will allow it and the expenditure of money meets your priorities as we discussed in tip number one. I guarantee that this simple, childish trick will reduce your impulse buying significantly if you will only stick to it.

5. Buying Quality Stuff

The old cliché that you get what you pay for is pretty accurate. Buying quality stuff may cost a little more, but it will last longer and save you money in the long run. Carefully evaluate every purchase, and buy the best quality you can afford that still allows you to stay within your budget. As many *Consumer Reports* side-by-side tests have shown over the years, the most expensive item is not always the best quality. Spend your money wisely, and invest only in quality stuff that will bring you years of enjoyment.

Once you purchase quality stuff, take care of it! If you are going to spend more of your hard-earned money on something of quality, you must also invest the time necessary to take care of it. Taking care of your quality purchases saves you money in the long run by not having to replace the item as often. In addition, taking care of your assets improves your quality of life. We will cover this later in the book.

6. Give Yourself a Raise

For every reoccurring expense you eliminate, in essence, you give yourself a raise. Think about it. If you are spending money regularly on a purchase you made, eliminating this payment frees up money in your budget and is as good as getting a raise from your employer. For example, let's say that you purchased a car two years ago on an installment loan at 4 percent interest. Every month the payment comes due for $245. If you can find a way to pay off this purchase early—maybe with cash from your long-term saving account—you effectively give yourself a $245 a month raise. In addition, you avoid some of the interest you would have had to pay.

For every expense you avoid, you give yourself added purchasing power. In financial terms, this is called cost avoidance. For example, if you normally spend $13 every two weeks to wash your car and you decide to do it yourself or find a place that will wash your car for $7, every penny you save increases your purchasing power by that amount through avoiding or reducing an expense. Increasing your purchasing power by avoiding unnecessary expenses improves the bottom-line of your budget and allows you to shift more of your money to the important things that matter to you most.

7. Pay Your Bills on Time

Paying our monthly bills on time is essential to maintaining our budget and staying on track with our Financial Means Plan. The best way I have found to do this is by setting up a "tickle file." A tickle file is a filing system that helps "tickle" our brain when something needs doing. In this case, a tickle file helps us keep our bills organized.

Setting up a tickle file is easy. Start by labeling thirty-one file folders "one through thirty-one" and put them in an empty drawer of your desk or wherever you pay your bills. Each file folder represents one day of the month.

As bills come in through the mail, determine their due dates and then count back seven days from that date. For example, if a bill comes in with a due date of March 25th, count back seven days to March 18th, and write that date on the outside of the envelope. This date (March 18th) represents the day that the bill must be processed by you to make sure it has time to get to the person you owe by the due date. Why do we do this? We do this because, if you normally pay your bills by check through the mail, the seven days will provide the payment plenty of time to travel through the mail to its destination.

Once you have gone through all of your bills and marked them with a date seven days before it is due, it is time to file them away into our tickle file we created with our thirty-one file folders. Filing your bills away depends on your schedule. When do you normally pay your bills? I suggest that if you are not already paying your bills once a week, you should start doing it right away. Paying your bills only once a week decreases the time you spend paying bills, reduces your overall stress, and simplifies your life. I think that sitting down and paying your bills only once a week is good for your mental health.

Let's say you want to pay your bills on Monday. Take the envelopes you just marked with a date that is seven days before the due date and file them away in the corresponding Monday folder in your tickle filing system. For example, if the date you wrote on your envelope is March 18, 2014, and that is a Tuesday, move back to the nearest Monday (March 17th) and file the bill in the file folder labeled "17." If the envelope date is March 17th, since the seventeenth is a Monday, and that is the day you pay bills, file it in the file folder labeled "17." If the envelope date is March 27th, move backward to the closest Monday (March 24th) and file the bill in the folder labeled "24." Keep following this process until all of your bills are filed.

Every Monday, when it's time to sit down and pay your bills, open the file folder that corresponds to that Monday and pull out all the bills you filed away. We know that every bill there is seven days or more away from its due date. If we write the bills and send them out on Monday, we know that each payment has plenty of time to reach its destination before it is due.

If paying bills on Monday doesn't work for you, use whatever day is best for you. Whatever day you decide on, use the same process of counting back seven days from the due date, move backward from that date, and file it away in the folder that corresponds to the day that you process your payments. For example, if you normally pay your bills on Thursday, instead of filing them on the date that Monday falls on, file them in the file folder labeled with Thursday's date. If you pay your bills on Wednesday, file your bills in the corresponding Wednesday file folder. It really doesn't matter what day you use. The process is the same and keeps you paying your bills on time.

The tickle filing system is a simple process to follow to make sure our bills are always paid on time. It also works with paying our bills electronically. Paying our bills on time stops late payment penalties and interest payments. It also increases our credit rating and makes it easier the next time we want to buy something on credit. Most of all, it allows us to live life more simply and keeps our Financial Means Plan on track.

Summing It All Up

Living within our means is one of the most important things we can do to keep our lives on track. It keeps us focused on important things. It reduces stress in our lives because we know we can pay our bills when they come due. It frees up time in our lives to spend on more important things. Living within our means is essential to living a simple life.

Once we have identified our life's priorities, creating our Financial Means Plan takes living within our means to the next level by making us dive deeply into our financial weeds to look at how we are spending our money. It clearly identifies, maybe for the first time, where our money is really going and whether it is truly supporting our priorities. Creating a Financial Means Plan allows us to refocus our spending on the things that make our lives worth living.

To create a Financial Means Plan, we used the 70-30 Financial System to create a budget. This process allows us to refocus our income on the things in our lives that matter the most to us by setting investment goals and spending limits. Seventy percent of our gross income supports the necessities of life, the basis for existence. Spending here is used to support the basic or first-level needs of day-to-day living, such as food, shelter, clothing, and any other expense necessary for survival itself.

We should spend 30 percent of our gross income investing in ourselves and others. Ten percent of this category is used on our second-level needs to add fun in our lives and to give our lives meaning and purpose. We should use this money as much as possible to support our priorities drawn from the four priority lists we created earlier. Our priorities are where we find true happiness and purpose in our lives.

The second ten percent of our gross income goes into our short-term savings and long-term investments. Five percent of that belongs in a savings account earmarked for unplanned expenses and emergencies. As we all have experienced, sometimes things happen outside of our control and catch us off guard at the worst possible times. The money invested in this account will remove the burden and added stress from our lives.

The second 5 percent is invested in our future in retirement plans such as a 401(k), an annuity, or any other long-term investment strategy that gives us financial stability in the twilight years of our lives. Whether we like it or not, old age is creeping up on all of us. Every day all of us are one day closer to retirement. We should invest 5 percent of every paycheck in a secure, long-reaching account that supports our future.

The final ten percent of this category is used to invest in others through charities and gifts. Investing in others is one of the best ways to not only support the community that surrounds us and make it a better place to live, but giving money to others is a proven way to bring happiness to our lives. Investing in others is not only a good investment, it is essential to our happiness and wellbeing.

Now that you have reduced the influence of unrealistic want on your life and decisions, defined your priority lists, and established your Financial Means Plan, you are over halfway to completing your Simple Life Plan and living the simple life you dream about. The next step of the process is establishing your Time Means Plan.

Step Four: Establishing Our Time Means

Time is the most valuable asset in the world. Nothing is more valuable. Wealth, power, and status fall well short of the value of time.

How valuable is time? To understand its value, let's look at the value of money. Let's pretend that you are the richest person in the world and that you can buy anything you want. Expensive cars, houses, boats, airplanes—anything you want to buy—are all well within your financial resources. In fact, you are so wealthy that if you want something, you just buy it. You don't even consider how much the item costs. Do you think $500 trillion would provide the purchasing power we are describing?

Now let's look at the value of time. Since we have established ourselves as having more purchasing power than most countries, let's look at the value of time and compare it to our wealth. Let's say you or I wanted to buy an extra thirty minutes each day to help us get everything done. How many times have we all said that we wish we had more time? We say, "I just don't have enough time to get (insert your task here) done." So, how much do you think an extra thirty minutes a day would cost? Could you or I buy thirty minutes with $500 trillion and make our day twenty-four hours and thirty minutes long? Of course not, you nor I nor anyone else can buy thirty minutes of time. Even if we had all the money in the world, we still couldn't buy one extra second. Time is so valuable we can't put a price on its significance.

As I'm sure many of you are tired of me saying, life is short. Forgive me, but I am going to keep saying it until we all understand how short life truly is. At birth, people in the United States have an average life span of just over seventy-eight years.[34] If we are lucky, we will die of old age, happy with where we've gone in life and how we've spent our time getting there. Unfortunately, for some of us, a tragic accident or an incurable disease will shorten our lives.

As we all know from experience, life can be going great today, and it can be gone tomorrow. Forgive me for being so morbid, but the time we have on this earth is a precious commodity much more valuable than all the money in the world. We have only one shot at life, a short span of time measured in days and years, to do the things that give our lives meaning and bring us happiness. Therefore, we must make sure we spend the limited amount of time that we've been given on this earth focusing on the priorities that bring purpose to our lives.

Although it is impossible for us to buy an extra second of time, we can spend our time without even thinking about it. We spend twenty-four hours every day of the total time allotted to us. While we spend some of this time productively meeting our life's goals and keeping us happy, we waste much of it. Every day when we're allocating our time for the day, please keep in mind that once a second is spent, it is gone forever. It can never be recaptured. There is no getting it back. No doing things differently. Once our time is spent, it's gone forever.

Worse yet, short of dying, there is nothing we can do to stop our time from being spent. All of us get twenty-four hours every day to make the most of our lives and to mold them into the lives we want. How we spend this time determines how successful and happy we are with our lives, which is why we must spend our time wisely and make the most of the time we have.

How are you spending your time? Are you happy with how you've spent your allotted time so far? Are you spending your time in a way that is taking you where you want your life to lead? If not, why not?

If you could look into the future and know that you only had ten years to live, would you change the way you live your life? What if you knew you had only five good years to accomplish your goals? Would you change the way you do things? What about three years? Would you change anything? If you answered no, then congratulations! You obviously have your priorities straight, and you are living your life in a way that gives you satisfaction. However, I suspect most of us want more out of life.

Just like money, how we spend our time is a good indicator of what is really important to us. Are you spending your time on the important things in your life? Are you spending your time focusing on the people and activities that mean the most to you? Are you spending your time accomplishing all of your goals and living your life as you dreamed it would be?

Life is too short. Each of us is ultimately responsible for living every second of our lives in a way that makes us happy and fulfills our dreams. We are responsible for how our lives are lived. If we are not living the lives we have always dreamed about, it's our own fault and we should do something today to get started doing what we know we should be doing.

Time is truly your most valuable asset in the world. Don't waste it. Keep your time focused on the important people, activities, and things in your life that meet your life goals. Use your remaining time concentrating on the things that give your life meaning and bring you happiness.

Just like our financial resources are budgeted in our Financial Means Plan, our time resources must be allocated in our Time Means Plan. We must look at how we spend our time just as we spend our money. Whereas our Financial Means Plan places limits on how we spend our money as it relates to supporting our priorities, a Time Means Plan assists us in determining how we spend our limited time resources to support the important things in our lives. Establishing our Time Means Plan is crucial to our success and happiness.

How do we establish a Time Means Plan? We must follow a two-step process. First, we must identify where we are spending our time. Second, once we have a handle on where our time is being spent, we must capture any time we can free up and reallocate it to our priorities.

The best way to determine how we spend our time is through a time study, a proven technique employed throughout the world to track how people use time and where time can be saved.

What is a time study? In the traditional sense, a time study is a method to record how long it takes to accomplish a task or a series of tasks. Frederick Winslow Taylor made the time study popular in the early 1900s.[35] He developed the technique to measure how long a worker takes to accomplish his or her particular job. Through this collection of data, he determined the best and most efficient way to complete the job to maximize each worker's time.

Using a variation of Mr. Taylor's method, we are going to establish a baseline of how we spend our time each day. The information we collect will be analyzed to determine not only how we are spending our time each day, but whether it is being used to support our priorities. We will use Our Time Means Plan to allocate our time to help us stay focused on the important people, activities, and things that give our lives meaning.

I challenge you to pick a typical week and track how you spend your time over seven consecutive days. For seven straight days, I want you to account for every fifteen minutes of time you spend throughout the day. If you're talking on the phone, write down talking on the phone. If you're watching TV, log that time as watching TV. If you're at work or sleeping, or even sleeping at work, write down whatever you are doing in fifteen-minute increments.

One word of caution—be honest with yourself. As humans we tend to fudge the truth and change our behavior when we think others are watching us. It is human nature to skew the results of our time study a little to make us look better than we sometimes deserve. Resist the temptation to do this. No one will ever see your time study unless you share it. Be honest with yourself so you can get an accurate accounting of how you spend your time each day. The more accurate your log, the better you will be able to manage your time later. If you diligently work to make your collection of data as complete as you can, I think you will be surprised at what you learn.

Your time collection worksheet should be laid out with each hour of a twenty-four-hour day, broken down into fifteen-minute increments. You should account for every fifteen minutes of every hour for seven consecutive days and log them on your worksheet. Use one worksheet for each day of the seven-day study. See Figure 1 for an example of a few hours of a time collection worksheet. Your time collection worksheet should include all twenty-four hours of the day. You can go to Simple Life Publishing's website at www.SimpleLifePublishing.com and download a formatted time collection worksheet if you would rather not design your own.

At the end of your seven days, evaluate where you spent your time. If it helps you to organize the information into categories like work, sleep, or commuting time, and sum up the total time, feel free to do so. Organize the collected information in any manner that helps you fully understand how you are spending your time.

What are the goals of the time study? The goals are twofold. First and foremost, I want us to understand how we are spending our time. If time is truly our most valuable asset, we need to understand fully how we spend it. Just as we do with our financial information, we need to know where every second is spent and determine whether we are using it to support our priorities.

Quite frankly, when I completed my time study, I was shocked at how much time I spent on some activities, especially watching TV. I was obviously addicted to television and didn't even know it. I was also shocked at how little I slept each night. Most experts say you need seven to eight hours of sleep to function properly.[36] I was getting only five to six hours per night. No wonder I was tired all the time and had trouble focusing on occasion. To catch up on my sleep, I took long naps on the weekend, wasting my unallocated free time. Conducting a time study was an eye-opener for me, and I expect it will be an eye-opener for you too.

The second and equally important goal of the study is to help us identify time we are wasting on activities that do not contribute to our priorities or happiness. These time wasters are usually attributed to two things. First, they are the result of over committing or the inability to say "no." Or two, they are planned or unplanned activities that took longer than anticipated.

In my particular case, it was the TV. I was unwilling to turn it off, and as a result, it kept me awake at night, depriving me of the sleep I desperately needed. To help reduce the time I spent watching TV, my wife and I now record all our favorite programs on our DVR, and we never watch anything live. We skip through the commercials and save twenty minutes for every hour show, and ten minutes in a thirty-minute program. With movies, we sometimes save an hour or two just skipping through the commercials. We are usually a day behind on watching our shows, compared to everyone else, but the time we save is well worth the inconvenience of watching it a day late.

The overriding goal of our time study is to recognize and understand how we spend our limited time and eliminate activities that keep us away from our priorities and limit our happiness. Focusing our money and time on our priorities—people, activities, and things—that give our lives meaning is crucial to our well-being and will bring happiness to our lives beyond measure.

Figure 1

TIME	ACTIVITY
5:00 AM	
5:15 AM	
5:30 AM	
5:45 AM	
6:00 AM	
6:15 AM	
6:30 AM	
6:45 AM	
7:00 AM	
7:15 AM	
7:30 AM	
7:45 AM	
8:00 AM	
8:15 AM	
8:30 AM	
8:45 AM	
9:00 AM	
9:15 AM	
9:30 AM	
9:45 AM	
10:00 AM	
10:15 AM	
10:30 AM	
10:45 AM	
11:00 AM	
11:15 AM	
11:30 AM	
11:45 AM	
12:00 PM	

What did John and Kristina find out from their time study? Like most of us, they found out that they were not getting enough sleep, spending too much time watching TV, and wasting a lot of time on unimportant activities. However, most surprisingly, they discovered how much time they were spending driving to and from work each day. John is spending over two hours each day round trip. Kristina is spending over an hour and twenty minutes traveling back and forth to work. Together, they are spending about seventeen hours a week commuting to and from work. That is equivalent to over thirty-five days a year. To see their completed time collection worksheets, go to Simple Life Publishing's website.

What must John and Kristina do? How do we, like John and Kristina, take control of our time? We use our Time Means Plan.

Our Time Means Plan consists of three basic premises: First, spend as little time as necessary on activities that support our Financial Means Plan. Who wants to spend all their time working to support their spending habits? We must try to find a balance in our lives by maintaining realistic financial goals that will keep our priorities in line with the work time required to achieve them.

Second, spend the maximum amount of time on activities that keep us close to our priorities and make us happy. Remember our priority lists? This is where we want to spend as much time as we can. Here is where we find happiness in our lives. Spending time here is where we get our biggest bang for our time.

Finally, eliminate time spent on things that do not support our priorities, our finances, or our happiness. These are the big timewasters of life and are specifically addressed in the final step of our Simple Life Plan process, decluttering our lives. We will spend more time on this step in the next chapter. During this step, we will reduce or eliminate everything we can. The time we save here will free up time for more important priorities.

So what did John and Kristina do about the time they spend commuting each week? John is going to take advantage of his company's Work from Home Program and will spend two days a week working from home. In addition, on the days he must go into work, he is going to commute by public transit and let someone else do the driving. Come to find out, there is a bus stop just two blocks from their house that will drop him off a block from his office. Not only will this change save John a significant amount of money on gas and parking fees and wear and tear on his automobile, he can now use this time more productively working on his job search and checking on family and friends with his smartphone.

Kristina took the same approach as John and looked for ways to use her commuting time more productively. Kristina checked around her office and discovered three other women who live within several blocks of their home. Kristina reached out to them and invited them to join her for a cup of coffee. After talking, they all agreed they were spending too much time and money commuting to work, and they agreed to share the load by carpooling. Under their new plan, each woman agrees to drive one week a month for the good of the group. Not only will Kristina reclaim some of her time she spends driving to and from work that now can be used more productively, she has added three new friends at her office.

We all have the same amount of time to spend each day. We must be diligent with our time and use it wisely. Why? Because once our time is spent, it is gone forever. We can't buy more time, nor can we reclaim any of it after it is gone.

In the next few pages, we will discuss several general time-management tips that we should try to incorporate into our Time Means Plan. Just as we discussed in the Financial Means Plan section of the book about money management, there are excellent books on the market about time management, and I encourage everyone to invest a little time reading one. Sometimes doing the simplest of things will make a huge difference in how we spend our time and will free up time for the more important things in our lives.

Learn to Say No

For most people *no* is the first word we learn to speak. As children, we use this word relentlessly when we want to show our disapproval about something we are being asked to do. Children don't give a second thought to using the word *no* when they feel it is appropriate.

Unlike children, adults are often more reluctant to use the word *no*. We sometimes feel that by saying no we let someone down or give up the opportunity for future benefits that would result from saying yes. This is crazy thinking.

Our time is the most valuable asset we have, and we should protect it with our lives. We wouldn't give our hard-earned money to an unworthy cause; neither should we give our time to something that is not worthy of our time.

In addition, we shouldn't feel like we need to give an excuse for saying no. The phrase "Just Say No" was not only a good drug campaign conducted by the federal government several years ago, it also applies to our time. Never feel pressure to give an excuse for saying no. Our time belongs to us, and we should spend it as we see fit. However, we don't want to be rude like a child might be. When we say no, we should say, "I'm sorry, but I can't participate," and don't say anymore. Giving an excuse only opens us up for an awkward follow-up encounter if the excuse given goes away or is later removed or withdrawn. If the request of our time doesn't meet our Time Means Plan goals, just say no and move on.

Automate Whenever It Makes Sense

Anything we can automate, but still keep control of, we should do. Automatic bill payment, medication refills, deliveries, and direct deposit on checks are the first things that come to mind. In my own case, I spent an hour or so every Sunday night going through the bills in my tickle file writing checks and addressing envelopes. At first, I was concerned that I wouldn't have the money in my checking account to cover the automatic payments as they hit their due dates. I felt by paying by check, I had more control over my expenditures when I released the money for payment.

Guess what? I was wrong. Modern banking systems are much more advanced than I first thought. Automating our bill payments does not sacrifice our ability to control the distribution of our money. In fact, it will lessen our time dealing with payments, and it will save us money by not having to buy so many of those increasingly expensive postage stamps. In my opinion, that is a win-win.

So if there is something in your life you can automate, you should seriously consider doing it. The time and money you can potentially save is well worth the effort going forward.

Delegate Whenever Possible

Along the same lines of automating, we should delegate tasks whenever possible. Delegating is like multitasking. When someone else completes a task for us, it frees up time for us to focus on other, more important, tasks. It allows us to complete more work than we would have otherwise been able to accomplish.

However, when we delegate, we must be sure to select the right person for the job. Picking the wrong person may not only add extra time to completing the task, but may result in an unacceptable outcome. Picking the right person is critical to reducing our time spent on a task and increasing our multitasking efficiency.

If we can't find the right person to delegate a task to, and if it makes sense, pay a professional to do it. Sometimes a task requires special skills or tools that we may not have or not want to invest in. There may be tasks we have no interest in or just don't want to do.

A task that fits in this category for me is changing the oil in my car. Changing the oil regularly is important and prolongs the life of the car. I can do it, and I have done it many times in the past, but I'm not convinced that I can purchase the supplies to do it myself cheaper than I can have someone else do it for me. As a result, I made the choice several years ago to pay someone else to change the oil in my car. Paying someone else do it is a better use of my time, and it frees me up to do other things.

I'm sure there are tasks you hate doing or you don't have the skills to do yourself. If it makes sense, pay someone else to do them for you. Paying someone else frees up valuable time for your priorities and gives you time to do things that make you happy.

Make Lists and Stick to Them

It is a fact that if we make a list and stick to it, we will not only eliminate impulse buying and save money, we will also save time. There is nothing like going to the mall and wandering aimlessly from store to store looking for a bargain. For some people, an expedition from store to store is an adventure. For me, it is an exercise in futility, and I hate it. When I do this, I end up spending more money than I intended to spend, and I throw away—yes I said throw away—valuable time playing the game the retailer plays to get me to spend more of my hard-earned dollars.

For those of you who feel visiting every store in the mall on a regular basis is something that makes you happy and gives meaning to your life, that's okay, but please be careful. If spending your valuable time in the mall makes you happy and is one of your priorities, please continue to have fun, but make sure you put limits on yourself to keep focused on your Simple Life Plan. I recommend that you go to the mall with a list and try to limit yourself to the items you have identified. Making a list and sticking to it is the best way to put limits on your spending and your time.

If fact, we should make lists for everything. We should make a list before we go to the grocery store. We should make a list for the errands we need to run. We should make a list for the tasks we need to complete today. Spending a little time making a list and focusing on it will not only save us huge amounts of time in the long run, it will make us more productive by focusing us on what we have identified as important.

Before we finalize our list, we must carefully look at the list and eliminate all the items that are not absolutely necessary. Prioritize the remaining items from A to Z. A list can be not only a time-saver, it can also be a time-waster if it includes things that are not important to our overall goals. These items, if we let them, will get us off track and send us down a path that might keep us from getting our important items completed.

Finally, putting more items on our list than can possibly be completed in our allotted time frame will only add stress to our lives. Put only important items on our list that can be completed in the amount of time we have allocated. When we're finished with the list, throw it away. It has served its purpose and saved us time and maybe some money too.

Do Things Only Once

The old saying "Do things right the first time" is a great philosophy to follow. Nothing wastes time more than doing something twice because we didn't do it correctly the first time. If we're going to invest our valuable time in any activity, we must make sure we do our homework and do it right. Any work that is less than acceptable requires us to tackle the task again later. Having to do anything more than once is not only frustrating and stressful, it wastes time that could have been spent doing something else.

If the task is one that others depend on, failing to complete it correctly could also tarnish our reputation. Nobody likes working with people who do less-than-desirable work. Having to pull the weight of those who are not doing what they should be doing makes completing a task harder on every person involved and increases everyone's time investment. Shoddy work is the quickest way to destroy our character and cause people to avoid working with us.

In addition to doing things right the first time, we must make a practice of touching things only once. When we begin a task, we shouldn't stop until we have finished. Never start the task, put it down, and come back to it later. Every time we have to return to a task we didn't finish, we waste our time. Touching things more than once adds time to the overall task and reduces our productivity.

This way of thinking can be applied to everything we do. For example, when we paint a room of our house and stop before we finish, what happens? If the job drags on for multiple days we have to clean the brushes multiple times, we keep the room in a state of disarray, and we can't use it as it was intended. We have to mix the paint numerous times and end up spending time doing other tasks over and over until we finish the job. Before we start any job, we must make sure to give ourselves enough time to not only do it right the first time, but enough time to touch the task only once.

Unsubscribe from Things We Don't Need

Every day our mailboxes are filled with items begging for our attention. Advertisements, product samples, and junk mail are just some of the things we drag into the house every afternoon when we get home from work. Granted, most of these items were sent to us without our knowledge and can't be stopped, but if they can be eliminated, do so. We waste countless hours a year going though this information for little return on the time investment made.

At the least, we should stop at the garbage can each day on our way into the house and throw away everything we have no interest in. Don't even take the time to open the envelope if it provides no value to our lives.

Throw it away immediately. We should not allow junk to sit on our countertops and force us to touch it again later. We have wasted enough time on it already. Get rid of it!

We should reevaluate from time to time the items we receive in the mail that we have requested. We all have subscriptions to newspapers, magazines, and other material that give us pleasure. On a regular basis we must make sure these subscriptions are still providing value and are worthy of our time. If they're not, cancel the subscriptions and get rid of them. Once the pleasure is gone, they just collect dust in our magazine rack and cause us more work later when they get in our way of finding something we need.

In addition, when we are finished reading the paper or our magazine, we must throw it away. The thought that we may go back to an article and read it again sometime in the future is only wishful thinking. Nine times out of ten we will never go back to it. It will only add clutter to our lives.

If you don't believe me, try this. The next time you have this feeling after reading your favorite magazine, write the date you read it on the cover before you put it away. Every time you pick it up to reread an article from this point forward, write that date on the front cover. Mark your calendar for three months from now and, on that date, go back to where you stored the magazine—if you can find it—and check the dates written on the cover. If it still only has the original date, throw the magazine away. If you haven't gone back to it in three months, face it, you are never going back. Get rid of the magazine and make room for something important in your life.

Reducing the clutter of our old periodicals saves us time in the long run by not having to keep them neat and orderly. It also reduces our time of having to move them out of the way when we need to look for other things. We will spend more time on this in the next chapter.

Do Your Most Difficult Tasks on Your Time Schedule

We all have times of the day when we are more productive. Some people are morning people while others are night owls. We must understand what times of the day we are more focused and productive and use these times to tackle our most difficult tasks. The worst thing we can do is try to accomplish a task when our hearts and spirits are not into it.

We must keep attuned to our body's clock because, over time, our regulator may change. When I was younger, I was a night owl, and I did my best work when everyone else was asleep. As I got older, my body clock flipped, and my most productive time of the day is now before lunch. It is important to be aware of our body's clock and adjust our schedule so that when we have difficult tasks to accomplish, we plan them for the most productive times of our day. Nothing is worse than trying to complete a task when our body will not cooperate. We end up spending our time daydreaming about what we would rather be doing. We must always listen to our biological clock and abide by what it is telling us.

In summary, time is truly our most valuable asset. Spend it wisely. We already possess all the time we have been promised. We must keep our time concentrated on the important people, activities, and things in our lives that meet our life's priorities. We must use the strategy of our Time Means Plan to keep us focused on the things that give our lives meaning and happiness.

Managing our resources, both money and time, finishes the fourth step of our Simple Life Plan. Once we have identified our priorities, taken control of our finances with our Financial Means Plan, and refocused our time to give it the importance it deserves through our Time Means Plan, we can now start to live our lives more simply by improving our quality of life. The next and final step of living the simple life you dream about is being attentive to improving our quality of life through decluttering our relationships, activities, and stuff. Turn the page and let's get started.

Step Five: Decluttering Our Lives

To this point, we have completed four of the five steps to living the simple life you dream about. In step one, we eliminated the influence of unrealistic wants by developing a strong core-value system. A strong core-value system allows us to evaluate the outside influences that distract us every day competing for our resources. In step two, we identified our priorities. Here, we identified all the people, activities, and things that are important to us. In step three, we put in place a strategy that allows us to manage how we spend our money through our Financial Means Plan. By living within our means, we can keep our money focused on our priorities. In the fourth step, we developed our Time Means Plan. With this process, we evaluated how we spend our time every day so that we can find ways to refocus it on the people and activities that are important to us. The final and equally essential step in living the simple life you dream about is improving our quality of life by decluttering our lives.

Most experts would agree that, to improve one's quality of life, we have to start by improving our health through eating right, exercising, and reducing our stress. The themes we encounter most often are losing weight, reducing our alcohol consumption, and smoking cessation. Although all of these things are important to improving one's quality of life, that's not what I am talking about here. Improving our quality of life, in my opinion, begins with simplifying the way we live our lives.

Just like improving our health, simplifying our lives is a key factor in the quality of life we live. Simplifying our lives can be realized only by turning off the influence that unrealistic wants has on us and our decision making. Once we turn off the influence—the pressure of acquiring more things than we really need—unrealistic wants can be eliminated from our lives. This added pressure to acquire more than is really necessary happens when we allow people to manipulate us and talk directly to our unrealistic wants gene.

When we give people access to us, they inundate us with messages that try to convince us that more of something is always better. Truthfully, more is not always better. In fact, most often, living under the "more is always better" mentality will completely disrupt our lives and take us away from the people, activities, and things that are important to us.

True happiness comes through simplifying the way we live our lives and incorporating the people, activities, and things that are important to us. Happiness has never been about how much we have or can acquire, but it comes through how we live our lives and the satisfaction life brings us.

Not only is more not always better, but less is more. Yes, less is more. How can less be more? Actually, it's quite simple. Too much of anything will complicate and clutter our lives by stealing our money, time, and quality of life from us.

How does having too much do this? Taking care of the extra stuff in our lives has a direct effect on our income requirements, time commitments, and our quality of life.

The Law of Diminishing Returns[37] perhaps explains this concept best. Although this law is most often used to explain productivity measures in the workplace, the law also illustrates that the more we have of something, the less valuable it becomes to us as we continue to acquire more of it. For example, let's pretend we just finished a three-mile run. We are tired and extremely thirsty. The first glass of water was incredible and took the edge off our thirst. The second glass of water wasn't as good as the first, but it still hit the spot. With each additional glass of water—the third, fourth, and fifth—our thirst decreases, and our desire for more water diminishes. By the end of the sixth glass, we can't drink another drop. Our desire for more water is so exhausted that someone could offer to pay us to drink the seventh glass, but we probably wouldn't do it. Why? The more water we drink, the less important it becomes to quenching our thirst and giving us pleasure—hence, the Law of Diminishing Returns. The more of something we have, the less important it becomes to us.

This law has a direct effect on every part of our lives. It affects our priorities, money, and time. It affects our relationships, activities, and stuff. Whenever we have more than we really need, the Law of Diminishing Returns explains how it takes control of our lives.

Let's use an example from an earlier chapter to illustrate this point. Owning a car is a wonderful thing. It gives us independence and the ability to come and go as we please. The basic model will take us anywhere we want to go. However, our need for more won't allow it. We must have more!

Why won't the basic model do? It doesn't have all the features we want. It doesn't have all the bells and whistles we have been convinced we must have. So what do we do? We buy the more expensive car. We reason that, because it has more features than the basic car, it must be better.

Have we ever stopped to consider the long-term effects this kind of decision has on our lives? It affects how we view our priorities, how we spend our money, and how we use our time.

It affects our priorities by confusing us about what is important. When we get into the "more is better" mentality, we sometimes lose sight of our real priorities and let our focus move to less important things. In this particular case, if we were looking only for a dependable car to get us back and forth to work every day, spending extra money on luxury items may have wasted our financial resources on extra stuff we may never use. Here we place more value on the car than it deserves. In extreme cases, our car can sometimes become more important to us than anything else in the world. If you don't believe this can happen, go to a car show or watch one on TV. Those cars are the most important thing in the world to the people who own them.

It affects our money by sometimes convincing us to spend more money than we should. When we purchase something that is more than we really need, it takes financial resources away from our priorities and prevents us from realizing others. How does it do this?

It only stands to reason that if you add features to an automobile, it will increase the base cost of the vehicle. But have you ever stopped to calculate the effect of real dollars that your decision has created? Don't feel too bad if you haven't. Most of us don't. We are usually too busy letting our "more is better" mind-set tell us how special the extra features will be.

Our decision to purchase a car that is more than we really need has a direct impact on our income requirements. With the basic model, we would have to free up only $290.00 per month for five years. This figure includes taxes, finance charges, and all the dealer add-ons. However, the car we ultimately select has a monthly cost of $475.00. When we buy the more expensive car, we commit $185.00 more per month or $11,100 over the life of the loan. This real number represents an income commitment we must guarantee the dealer and the lending bank that we will maintain throughout the term of the loan. More important, this number represents income we cannot use to support our other priorities. If we could turn off our "more than we really need" attitude, convince ourselves that we would be okay with fewer bells and whistles, and still remain happy with our purchase, we could save ourselves a considerable amount of money per month and over the term of the loan agreement.

The extra bells and whistles or the extra stuff, like everything we buy, have a direct effect on the level of income we must maintain. In our example, the less expensive car provided the same basic functionality as the more expensive car provided. It will get us wherever we want to go, granted with fewer luxuries, but it will still get us there. But how much extra stuff is enough? Is the difference in cost worth the perceived value gained? What will we have to give up or go without to afford the more expensive car? Buying the basic model would permit us to decrease our financial commitment and allow us to spend it on something else that we may have needed.

Having more of something than we really need not only has a direct effect on our priorities and financial commitment, it directly affects our time obligation. Think outside the box for a moment. What if the money we saved by not purchasing the more expensive car was used to help cover our basic needs or expenses and freed up time we didn't have to spend working and generating income? Maybe the extra money we saved by buying the basic car could have kept us from having to take on extra shifts at work or from having to look for a second job to cover the expenses we are now having trouble meeting. Wouldn't it be nice not to work so much and be able to free up more time for the priorities in our lives? Turning off the "more than we really need" mind-set gives us more options to live like we really want to: spending time on our priorities, simplifying our lives, and being happy. In this example, as in most cases, more is rarely better.

Although my example centered on the purchase of a car, I am not picking on the automobile industry. This discussion applies to any subject. The "more is better" logic can apply to everything in our lives. We see it in our relationships, the activities we're involved in, and all the stuff we acquire during our lives.

Our priority focus, financial expenditures, and time commitments are huge considerations whenever we add more to our lives, but have we ever stopped and considered how having more affects our quality of life? When we add more to our lives, our priorities sometimes get confused, and we lose focus. Remember the juggler at the circus trying to keep multiple balls in the air. How does he do it? He does it by quickly moving his focus from one ball to the next, never focusing on one ball too long. As more balls are added, his focus on each ball decreases as he moves faster to keep all the balls in the air. What happens when he gets distracted for even a second? All the balls come crashing to the ground.

Just like the juggler, when we add more to our already busy lives, we must move faster and faster just to keep our priorities in the air. We quickly move our focus from one priority to the next, never spending too much time on each one. The more we continue to add, the faster we have to move, and the less attention each priority gets. And then life happens. We get distracted. We lose focus on our priorities, and they all come crashing down. We miss an important deadline at work, forget an anniversary, or fail to pick up the kids after practice.

Just as it gets harder to focus on our priorities when we add more to our lives, the financial expenditures we must make to support this additional load also increases. Every relationship, activity, or thing we add has a direct cost associated with it. The money we commit to these "things" requires us to maintain a certain level of income to support the "more" in our lives.

How do we maintain a certain level of income to support the "more" in our lives? If we're lucky, we won the lottery or inherited a large sum of money from a rich relative. For most of us, we work every day. I don't know about you, but I really don't want to work every day. I want to spend my days focusing on my priorities, my passions, and being happy. Don't we all want this for our lives?

I think all of us would love to be in a financial position that would allow us to limit the time we spend working. But because of our sometimes overwhelming desire to acquire more things than we really need, we force ourselves to work more than necessary to maintain a level of income that supports our spending habits and the stuff we collect.

Worst yet, sometimes the financial commitments we make force us to work at jobs we hate. When this happens, the "more" in our lives begins to affect our time commitments. It's no secret, most of us dread getting up and going to work. To counteract the dread we most often feel, we resort to wishing our lives away by longing for the weekend to get away from the work we so dislike. We waste our valuable time working at jobs we despise so we can support the sometimes unnecessary spending we commit ourselves to, thinking it will make us happy. Isn't this sad? That's no way to live our lives, hating our job and wasting our lives away wishing for the weekend. Where is the quality of life in this?

If we could only turn off the "more" mentality and encourage ourselves to live with a little less and eliminate the extra stuff in life that we really don't need. Maybe then we could afford to work at a job that perhaps doesn't pay as well. Maybe we could work at a job that provides us the satisfaction we are looking for in a career, and we could look forward to going to work every day. You know what the experts say, "If you are lucky enough to have a job you love, you never work another day in your life."

But even more than wishing our lives away longing for the weekend, adding more to our lives directly affects our time commitments. For example, instead of using the automobile, let's look at purchasing a house. It only makes sense that the larger the house, the more successful we must be, right? We have been led to believe that having a large house is a sign of success. But is it?

One thing is for sure, the larger the house, the more resources it takes to maintain it. It takes more financial resources to heat it, cool it, furnish it, insure it, and pay the property taxes, just to name a few. In most cases, these costs relate directly to the size of the house. The larger the house, the more it costs.

Beyond the financial resources needed, the time commitment required to maintain the house also relates directly to its size. The larger the house, the more time it takes to vacuum the floors, clean the windows, dust the cobwebs, and do the many other things that must be done on a regular basis. The time commitment required to keep a large house presentable can be overwhelming if we don't have the resources available.

When we buy a house, like a car, we commit time resources to our purchase. It goes without saying that when we buy more house than we really need, we waste our limited time resources. We waste time we could have committed to more important priorities than maintaining a house. To me, success should not be measured by how much stuff we have accumulated or how large our house may be. In my opinion, we should measure success by how we use our limited resources to maintain our life's priorities and find the true happiness we seek.

Unfortunately, most often, we let our "more is always better" mind-set control how we approach our lives and we let it trick us into believing that more is the secret to being happy. Don't be fooled. More will never make us truly happy unless the "more" we are talking about supports our priorities in life, the things we have identified that make us happy in the first place.

Think about this. Who wants to spend their limited resources taking care of the things that represent the "more than we really need" in our lives? The "more" here can be almost anything we have too much of, such as unfulfilling relationships, over commitments to activities that bring no value to our lives, or the stuff we continue to collect that occupies our space and time. Too much of anything will clutter our lives and cause us to lose focus on the important things in our lives. Is this how we want to spend our limited resources, taking care of the clutter in our lives?

I break clutter down into three types: relationships, commitments, and stuff. Let's look at each one.

As difficult as this may be to admit, sometimes we make relationships more valuable than they really are. We all have relationships that clutter our lives and affect our quality of life. Some of these relationships are forced on us by where we work or through mutual friends. Others are voluntary relationships we entered into that we thought would add value to our lives, but now we feel trapped. Some are even long-term relationships we keep hanging onto for no good reason, like a bad penny.

Despite how these relationships came about, the more relationships we have, the more time and effort it takes to maintain them. It is simple math. The more we have of anything, the more difficult it is to manage. Remember what the experts say about the ideal span of control? They say we are capable of efficiently managing only five to seven things at one time.

Here is the question we must answer and act upon: are there relationships in our lives that have run their course and need to be eliminated? How do we answer that question? We answer the question by categorizing our relationships in three ways: priority relationships, fringe relationships, and relationships to be eliminated.

Priority relationships are with the people we identified in our Important People Priority List. These are the people we want in our lives. These are the relationships we want our resources to support. Our goal with this group of relationships is to keep them as close to us as we can. They are relationships we have identified as important to our happiness. When allocating our limited resources, we should choose these people first.

Fringe relationships are with people who are not a priority in our lives, but who are still important to our happiness. These relationships sit just outside the ring of our priority relationships. For whatever reason, these people are still valuable to our happiness, but are not considered a priority in our lives. Try to limit this group of relationships to a span of control you are comfortable with. However, keep in mind, when a contact opportunity arises with a priority relationship, our fringe relationship always comes second.

Finally, there are relationships we must try to eliminate from our lives. If a relationship adds no value and is not one we identify as a priority or a fringe relationship, we should get rid of as many of them as we can and limit our contact with those we cannot eliminate. We should not waste any of our limited resources on these relationships. Our ultimate goal is to free our time so we can spend it on our important relationships, the people who give value and meaning to our lives. Remember, we should always keep the people who bring us happiness close and push away all the others. We don't need them cluttering our lives, so don't keep them around.

Just as we sometimes let relationships clutter our lives, we over commit ourselves and get trapped in activities that prevent us from spending time on our more important priorities. This kind of clutter also affects our quality of life.

I think this type of clutter can sometimes be explained by the Pareto Principle or the 80-20 rule. The 80-20 rule states, in its most basic form, that 80 percent of the effects come from 20 percent of the causes.[38] In this particular case, 20 percent of the people involved in anything do 80 percent of the work. Over committing ourselves to activities that bring no value to our lives will control our lives if we allow it to.

Think back throughout your life and see how this rule applies to you. Chances are if you have ever felt over committed to anything in your life, you were probably one of the 20 percent doing 80 percent of the work.

For me it usually revolved around church activities. In most churches, especially the ones I have attended, 20 percent of the members do 80 percent of the work. The 20 percent teach Sunday School classes, teach Bible studies, prepare food for socials, sing in the choir, or take part in just about any other activity necessary to run a church. As the rule states, 20 percent of the members—most often the same members—do 80 percent of the work.

Don't get me wrong. The church activities I am describing are important to the church, and someone has to do them. I'm glad people are willing to commit to these activities because if they didn't, in my humble opinion, the church would not exist.

However, the real problem I am trying to identify stems from the fact that once organizers identify us as one of the 20 percent, they will sometimes take the least path of resistance and ask the same people to do everything that comes along. Why do they do this? Because they know who will say yes. They have asked these people repeatedly, and they rarely say no. To reduce the pain of the recruiting process, they stop contacting the 80 percent and contact only the 20 percent who are more willing to commit their time to almost any effort. In the end, by asking those of us who can't seem to say no, the recruiter saves pain and time enlisting the same people over and over. The 20 percent who fall into this category quickly over commit to activities.

Although I encountered this rule most often in church duties, this rule applies to all activities that we may be committed to: little league baseball, dance class, school activities, work, or a bowling league. If you are one of these people, the 20 percent who seem to get involved in everything you are asked to do, you are more than likely over committed to some of them.

The next time we are asked to commit to an activity, we must refer back to our priority lists. We must make sure that whatever we are being asked to commit to is a priority in our lives. If it's not, we must gracefully say no. Being overcommitted to anything that is not a priority in our lives steals our limited resources and takes us away from the things that are important to us. We must always keep our commitments limited to our priorities if we are going to keep our lives simple, fulfilling, and happy.

The final category of clutter is our stuff. Having more stuff than we really need clutters our lives and directly affects our quality of life. How does this happen? We develop the "I may need this someday" mind-set or think "This might be worth something in a few years." What happens when we do this? We never get rid of anything. Stuff builds up around us, and it takes over our space and our lives. Have we ever considered how much time it takes to keep our stuff organized, clean, and presentable?

In addition, having too much stuff cluttering our lives also requires us to have more space than we really need to maintain it. There is an old saying that "Stuff will always find a way to fill the available space we have." I've found this statement to be true! If you don't believe me, empty a drawer anywhere in your home and see how long it takes to fill it back up. It's human nature to throw stuff into a drawer to get it quickly out of the way and out of sight.

The same is true of a closet or garage. If you have an empty closet, you will keep putting stuff in it until it is full. If you have a garage or storage shed with a little extra space, your extra stuff will fill every nook and cranny until it is bursting at the seams. Funny thing, our garage that we were so proud of when we first bought our home that was supposed to store only our car and keep it out of the weather, now is full of our stuff. Our car is sitting in the driveway because all of our stuff has taken its place in the garage. Am I right? If we have available space and we don't control and put limits on our clutter, our stuff will always find a way to take over our space, cost us more money than we want to spend, and steal our time away from our real priorities taking care of it.

Now don't let me confuse you. Some stuff is good. Some stuff is necessary for our happiness. Remember when we identified all the things that make us happy in our priority lists? This is not the stuff I'm talking about here. The stuff I'm talking about is the extra things that are not a priority in our lives, but only clutter it.

So what do we do about all this extra stuff? I like to employ a three-step strategy: sell it, give it away, or throw it away. This is how it works. First, identify every cluttered space in your life and begin to declutter it using this strategy. Pick the low-hanging fruit first by selecting the space where you will get the most return for your time and effort. If that space is your garage, start there. If it is a closet or a room of your house, begin there. It really doesn't matter where you start. Getting started decluttering your life is what's most important.

The goal of decluttering our lives is not to organize our extra stuff, but to eliminate it from our lives. Therefore, resist the temptation to organize the extra stuff and try to stay focused on eliminating it. How are we going to eliminate it? We are either going to sell it, give it away, or throw it away. If we can make a little money by selling it, we will, but our main goal here is to get the extra stuff we don't really need out of our lives so we can make room for the stuff that is more important to us or that is a priority in our lives.

As you go through the space you selected, make four piles. Make a sell pile for all the extra stuff that has real value. Include only the stuff that has a real value. If you think someone will buy it, put it in the sell pile and move on.

If the item doesn't have any real value, use the second method, and give it away. Is there someone you know who may want the item, or is there a charity that that would take it? If so, tag it with the name of the person or charity, and put that item in the giveaway pile.

Likewise, if the item has no value or there is no one to give it to, throw it away immediately. If you let it linger any longer than necessary, your mind will convince you to keep it. The item will start quietly calling your name, and you will not be able to part with it. Remember, keeping our extra stuff is not our goal here. We want our extra stuff out of our cluttered lives, cluttering someone else's life, or we want it in the landfill. As you go through your extra stuff, stick to the plan, and get rid of it!

Finally, make a pile for all the stuff you want to keep. These are the things you can't live without. This stuff is a priority in your life. Put these things in a safe place away from the other stuff you are trying to eliminate from your life.

Once you have gone through the first space and separated all the extra stuff to eliminate into the three categories, start getting rid of everything you have identified. If you haven't already taken the stuff to be thrown away to the curb for garbage pickup, do it first. You want this stuff as far away from you as possible. If you have to, cover it up so you can't look at what's out there. Believe me, it will find a way back into your life if you let it.

For the stuff that is in your sell pile, open an eBay or Craig's List account and put it up for sale. You can use the local newspaper or a yard sale, but I think more people will see your items if you distribute them through an online seller. Limit the time it is listed to a reasonable period. The online seller can give you help with determining the time limit. At the end of this period, if your item hasn't sold, either give it to someone or throw it away. Don't let it creep back into your space. Remember again, our goal is to get rid of our extra stuff. If it doesn't sell, get rid of it. If it sells, guess what? You just made a little money on something you didn't need anyway.

Next, give away the stuff you have marked as "give away" as soon as you can. Drop it off at your friend's house or local charity, and remove it from your sight as soon as possible. Just like the stuff you threw away, this stuff wants back into your life and, if you are not diligent, it will find a way back into your space. If for whatever reason the item can't be donated, kick it to the curb! Throw it away! Get rid of it! Why would you want to keep something that no one else wants? One final thought about donations to a charity: be sure to ask for a receipt for everything you donate. You may be able to use the value of the donation as a deduction on your income taxes.

Finally, once your extra stuff has been removed from the space you were working on, it is time to organize everything that is left. Don't try to organize your space until all your extra stuff is removed. Why wait? When you are down to the stuff that is important, only then will you have an idea of how it needs to be organized. If you try to organize your stuff as you're going through it, you will spend more time shuffling through the same stuff over and over, which will slow you down. You want to finish disposing of your extra stuff as quickly as possible so you won't be tempted to let something that should be disposed of return to your space. Stopping to organize slows down this process, so save organizing the stuff that remains until last.

Repeat this process on every space you have identified. It may take a little time to go through all your stuff, but it will be well worth it once you're finished. Getting rid of the clutter of your extra stuff improves your quality of life.

Believe me, if we have available time to fill, just like empty space in a drawer, others will always find a way to fill it if we allow them to. This principle also applies to money. If we have extra money, there will always be someone with his or her hand out looking for us to spend it on them. Bottom-line, if we don't control our life-space and never get rid of the things that clutter our lives, our quality of life will be reduced. The extra relationships, commitments, and stuff we allow into our space will not only clutter our lives, it will steal our resources as we spend more money or time maintaining things we really don't need. In addition, this clutter adds stress to our lives and directly affects our health. Most importantly, clutter takes us away from our priorities and makes true happiness almost impossible to achieve.

Knowing that the extra stuff or clutter in our lives steals our money and time, we must learn to right size or simplify our lives and find the right level of clutter that allows us to focus our money, time, and energy on our priorities. Focusing on our priorities allows us to find the simple life we are looking for and discover true happiness.

My Hope for You

What is our biggest challenge to living the simple life we dream about? Getting started! Transitioning from dreaming about how we wish we were living our lives to taking action is the first challenge we face. Ask anyone who has made the transition and he or she will tell you that the first step is the hardest; however, it gets easier with each successive step.

Now, I am not going to lie to you. There will be days when you will question your decision to change your life. There will be days when you think you have made a mistake and are seriously considering changing your life back to the way it was before. Don't do it! Stay the course! Don't let the little voice in your head appeal to your insecurities. Stay committed to finding and living the simple life you dream about.

How do we stay the course and live the life we dream about? I've broken the process down into five simple steps. The first step of the journey is eliminating the power of outside influences on our decision making. We must establish for ourselves, without the help of anyone else, what we really need to make us happy. We must move away from the effects unrealistic wants have on our lives and focus on the people, activities, and things that bring us happiness. During this step, we must ask ourselves this question: What do we really need to be happy? What is the bare minimum we need to acquire and maintain to be satisfied? Striving to obtain or maintain anything above this basic needs level distracts us and pulls us away from our priorities and wastes our limited resources. Remember, being satisfied is a prerequisite of being happy.

Second, we must define our priorities. We must identify the people, activities, and things that are important to us and give meaning to our lives. To do this, we break down our priorities and create lists in four categories: important people, things I want to do, things I know I should be doing, and things that make me happy. These four priority lists define the "things" that are important to us. By focusing on these four lists, we surround ourselves with all the people, activities, and things that give us the basis for being happy, being satisfied. Once we incorporate our priorities into our lives and turn off the influence that unrealistic wants has on our basic needs assessment, we begin to simplify our lives and take the first step toward finding true happiness.

Third, we must establish a plan to identify and allocate the financial resources required to support our priorities. If we don't support our priorities with our monetary resources, they won't be priorities for long. We complete this step through our Financial Means Plan. With this plan, we allocate our spending through the 70-30 System, so our limited resources are freed up to support our priorities. Just like the four priority lists we established, we need a financial system to help keep our spending focused on our priorities through established spending boundaries. This keeps our spending within our available financial resources and keeps us living within our means.

Fourth, just as we need to develop a solid money-management strategy, we must also establish a plan to manage our time more efficiently. Time is our most valuable resource in the world and should be treated as such. We accomplish this step of the process through our Time Means Plan. With this plan, we review how we currently spend our time and identify where our time can be reallocated.

Our time-management goals are threefold. First, we want to spend as little time as necessary on activities that support our financial strategy. Who wants to spend all of their time working? Second, we want to spend the maximum amount of time on activities that keep us close to our priorities. This is where we find happiness. Finally, we want to eliminate time spent on things that do not support our priorities, our finances, or our happiness. Keeping our time concentrated on the important people, activities, and things in our lives that we identified in our priority lists, keeps us connected to the "things" that provide us happiness.

The final step that keeps us on course to live the simple life we dream about is improving our quality of life. We accomplish this step by decluttering our lives of unnecessary relationships, commitments, and stuff. Here we learned that more of something is not always better. In fact, less is more. Too much of anything will complicate and clutter our lives. Maintaining relationships, commitments, and stuff we don't really need steals our money, time, and quality of life. In addition, this clutter adds stress to our lives and directly affects our health over time. Most importantly, clutter takes us away from the priorities in our lives and makes true happiness almost impossible to achieve.

We will realize many benefits by living a needs-based lifestyle, focusing our resources on our priorities, and decluttering our lives. By default, our lives get simpler. We're able to surround ourselves with the very things that make our lives worth living. More importantly, when we do this, true happiness, real happiness, comes naturally.

Second, living our lives this way allows our decision-making process to become much clearer. An unrealistic wants mind-set has a tendency to cloud our decision-making process by allowing unnecessary wants to become real needs. Focusing on our baseline happiness requirements helps us stay focused on what's really important in our lives and keeps us from wasting our limited resources.

Third, turning off the influence that unrealistic wants has on our lives improves our money-management skills. No longer will unrealistic wants influence our purchasing decisions. We will be able to set a realistic budget and stick to it. We will be able to save for a rainy day and not be caught off guard by unexpected expenses. Above all, turning off the influence of unrealistic wants allows us to focus our financial resources on the priorities in our lives.

Finally, just as focusing our financial resources on our real needs improves our money-management skills, focusing on our real needs frees up more time to spend with the important people in our lives. Remember what we said? True happiness comes through doing the things we love with the people we love. Unrealistic wants have a tendency, like with money, to control our time. Our culture leads us to believe that more of something is always better. Accordingly, as one desire is fulfilled, another is created. We are never completely satisfied.

Consequently, we spend our entire lives in search of and acquiring things that we think will make us happy, but they never do. Worse yet, during our search for happiness, we lose sight of our priorities—the people, activities, and things—that bring us happiness. Over time, the clutter we collected during our unsuccessful search for happiness begins to control our lives and affects our quality of life. Focusing on our real needs stops this process and allows us to make time for the important "things" in our lives.

But focusing on our real needs not only makes our lives better, it makes the world a better place to live. For example, if everyone would stay focused on his or her real needs, everyone's cost of living would be reduced. With companies around the world focused on their real needs, there would be no need for exorbitant prices to boost profits or out-of-control salaries to retain popular leaders. Companies would set prices and make profits on their products and services based on the companies' real needs.

In fact, everything on our planet would be better if everyone focused on their real needs. For instance, disease would be reduced or wiped out in the world. Finding cures and developing medicines to treat the sick would not depend on the market viability of a product before it was manufactured and administered.

Financial crises in the world would be eliminated. Everyone—including countries—would live within their means and not overextend their financial resources.

The family unit would be strengthened. People would have more time to spend with their loved ones and the important things in their lives.

Simply put, with just these few examples, the world would be a better place if everyone lived his or her life focused on his or her real needs. When you think about it, unrealistic wants affect our lives every day, in every corner of the world. Will the people of the world ever be motivated to focus only on their real needs? Probably not. As long as the influence of unrealistic wants controls the world we live in, we are doomed to the lives we are living.

We may not be able to change the world we live in, but we can make our lives better. Following the five-step process I have explained in this book is the start to living the simple life you dream about. By focusing our lives on our real needs and priorities, supporting our priorities with our resources, and decluttering our lives as we improve our quality of life, we can make our lives better. By following the five steps outlined in this book, we can simplify our lives and allow ourselves to find the real happiness we are searching for.

Remember when I told you about letting my unrealistic wants get the best of me in Pine Bluff, Arkansas? When I left my family to help a bag plant keep its doors open during a work dispute? Do you remember how I put myself and my family in danger and missed an important event in my son's life? Well, that wasn't the whole story. As Paul Harvey used to say, "Here is the rest of the story."

When I went to Pine Bluff, Arkansas, I didn't go alone. I had a good friend I worked with at the Franklin, Kentucky, plant who left for Pine Bluff two weeks before I did. Let's call him "Jimmy." He was a production supervisor and worked on the second shift.

Jimmy was a big fisherman. To say he had a passion for fishing is an understatement. He was driven by his dream of owning a fishing boat and relaxing on the lake in his off time. He knew what he wanted, and just like Tim "The Tool Man" Taylor, could spout out all the details of the boat. (Tim Taylor, played by Tim Allen, was the star of a hit TV show called *Home Improvement*.) The boat for Jimmy was a twin-hull, ninety-horsepower, four-cycle Mercury, with a depth finder, fish finder, and a five-horsepower trolling motor—arr, arr, arr! Unfortunately, Jimmy never knew Tim Taylor. They would have been great friends.

I met Jimmy in 1980 while attending our company's management program in Mount Vernon, Ohio. Jimmy worked for the same company I worked for, but in Franklin, Kentucky. I worked at the Florence, Alabama, plant. For one week each month, for six months, Jimmy and I spent time together.

I remember the first time I met Jimmy. It was in the Columbus, Ohio, airport. It was our first week at the school, and we were all instructed to meet at the airport to be driven up to Mount Vernon by the instructor and founder of the school. As I walked down the ramp of the plane to the waiting area, I saw Jimmy standing by an older gentleman holding the sign I was looking for. Jimmy was an extremely thin man about my age and height. He wore blue jeans and an old baseball hat. After I met the instructor, I was introduced to Jimmy.

As we waited for the others to arrive, we all went into a lounge area to talk. Being from Alabama, I worried about my accent and the ribbing I was sure to get. There were people from New York, Michigan, California, New Jersey, and Minnesota coming to the class.

But after hearing Jimmy speak the first time, I didn't fear the ribbing I anticipated any longer. Jimmy spoke with a southern drawl that so thick it made me sound as if I were from New York City. You could practically carry on a conversation between the words of his sentences. I never knew until then that some Kentuckians spoke that way. I thought that the people of Kentucky, a border state between the North and the South, would have more of a northern or neutral accent. I was wrong. For six weeks that year, Jimmy represented Kentucky to me and changed my whole perception of the state.

Jimmy and I became good friends during the six weeks we spent together. It was hard not to. We spent twelve to fourteen hours a day together as a group. We studied together. We cut up and laughed together. We went out after class together every night. Except for breakfast, we spent almost every waking minute together. Jimmy didn't like getting up in the morning and most days skipped that meal to get a little extra sleep.

I learned a lot about Jimmy during this time. I learned about his family. I learned about Kentucky and how everybody there doesn't talk like he did. According to him, their drawl was much worse than his. I learned the good and bad things about his plant in Franklin where he worked. I also learned about Jimmy's love for fishing.

Jimmy loved to fish. At times, that was all he wanted to talk about. He told me of his dream to own a nice boat and spend his off time fishing at the Land between the Lakes. This is a major camping and recreation area in western Kentucky between Kentucky Lake and Lake Barkley just east of Paducah. I must have heard about his dream a thousand times during that six-week period.

As kind of a graduation present, our last week of school was spent at the company's corporate headquarters in Seattle, Washington. It was a beautiful place. The building was built into the side of a hill with all types of vegetation planted on the different levels of the roof. The front of the building was glass and overlooked a small lake that had about twenty or thirty geese.

By the lake was the largest American flag I had ever seen up until that time. It must have stood fifty feet high and seventy feet wide. It was attached to a flagpole that must have been three feet in diameter. I must have taken ten to twelve pictures of the flag that week. Jimmy ribbed me every time I took a picture. He said that I acted as if I had never seen an American flag before, but I didn't care. I was so afraid that one of my pictures, of my film-based camera, would not turn out, and no one back home in Alabama would believe me.

That week was incredible. We met with corporate officers who explained the goals and mission of our company. We were shown top-secret research projects that our company was working on at the time. We were entertained every night at a nice restaurant around the Seattle area. The corporate office spared no expense on us that week and made us feel special about where we worked.

On our last full day in Seattle, officers took us to see the owner of the company's office. On the way up in the elevator, they told us that he was in town, and if we saw him in his office, just walk on by and pretend he wasn't there.

When the elevator doors opened, we walked into a large room with a huge tapestry hanging on a wall. It must have been 150 feet away on the opposite end of the room. It looked like a beautiful forest framed perfectly in the center of the wall. A pathway from the elevator to the tapestry drew your eyes to the picture. On each side of the path were plants of varying heights that separated the vice presidents' offices from one another.

As we walked down the path, we saw the company's owner to our left sitting at his desk. He was in the middle of a clump of plants about six feet high. Jimmy leaned over and whispered to me that we had come too far not to meet him and proceeded to part the plants and climbed into his office. Jimmy reached out his hand and introduced himself as our guide tried to stop him. Without pause, the owner stood up, shook Jimmy's hand, and invited the rest of us into his office. For the next thirty minutes, we casually talked to him while each of us in the class had our picture taken standing next to him. Thanks to Jimmy, all of us were able to meet our company's owner. To my knowledge, no other class ever did.

The next morning we left Seattle, and I didn't see Jimmy again for two years. The next time I saw Jimmy was when my plant in Florence, Alabama, closed and I went for an interview in Franklin, Kentucky.

I couldn't wait to see Jimmy again. All the members of our class had tried to stay in touch, but like many long-distance friendships, we gradually drifted apart. We lost touch with one other, and our calls to each other all but stopped.

As I walked up the sidewalk to the entrance of the Franklin plant, Jimmy met me at the front door. Jimmy hadn't changed a bit. The slender man I first met in Mount Vernon, Ohio, was still the same. I couldn't prove it, but I think he had the same baseball hat he had on the first time I met him.

We shook hands and caught up as quickly as we could before my interview. Jimmy still talked about fishing, and when I asked him if he had bought the boat he had always wanted, he said no and never gave a good reason when I asked him why. It was one of those things that he kept putting off, never making the commitment for, or freeing up the time to do. It was good to see Jimmy, and I hoped I would get the opportunity to work with him again.

My wish came true. I accepted a production scheduler's position and reported to work on the following Monday. The two years that followed my arrival at the Franklin plant were hectic. Of course, it could never be busy enough to keep Jimmy from talking about his love of fishing.

In October of 1983, just months after our son Jonathan was born, the company's only bag plant in Pine Bluff, Arkansas, started having contract negotiations with its local union. Within a few days, Jimmy was sent to Pine Bluff when the contract negations broke down. A strike was inevitable and the emergency plan was executed. People from all over the country converged on Arkansas to help save the plant.

Two weeks later, I got the call and went to work there as well. I flew into Little Rock, Arkansas, and was met at the airport by a Mrs. Thompson, the plant manager's secretary. After my bag never arrived at baggage claim, she drove me to the plant to meet the general manager.

After a short discussion, the general manager took me into the production area where Jimmy was the first person I saw. He was not the same Jimmy who left Franklin two weeks before. He looked tired, worn down, and barely smiled when I greeted him. As we stood and talked for a minute, I realized Jimmy was a changed man. He was no longer the happy-go-lucky person I used to know. I couldn't explain it, but he was different, and just like the angry crowd outside the plant, it scared me.

However stressful our situation was, Jimmy's love for fishing never went away. Not a day went by that he didn't mention it in some way. It took him away from the stress we were experiencing and took him to a place he dreamed about.

Only this time his talk about fishing was different. Jimmy made a commitment in Pine Bluff, Arkansas, to purchase the fishing boat and follow his dream, one that he had been putting off most of his life. He promised to spend more time relaxing on the lake he so loved. He was determined to make his dream of fishing in his new boat come alive when we returned home.

The situation we were in for those few months made all of us, including Jimmy, reevaluate our decisions to be there. Jimmy made a commitment and was determined to find a way to slow life down and live it doing the things he loved to do. One day, while we took a short lunch break, Jimmy leaned over to me and said, "Life is too short, and I am not going to put off buying that boat any longer." I agreed with Jimmy that we had all made a mistake coming here to work in the environment we were placed in because of the lure of a little extra money. Both of our lives changed that day.

From that moment forward, all I could think about was getting back home to my family. I missed them more than anything. Missing an important event in my son's life when he learned to sit up on his own was the final straw, and it weighed heavily on my mind. It was all I thought about. I couldn't sleep at night. I had to get home as soon as possible and right my wrong.

Jimmy reacted much differently than I did and began to scrimp and save every penny he made in Pine Bluff. The company paid us an additional fifteen percent above our regular salary, plus a daily allowance for food and sundry items while we were there. Jimmy never touched any of that money. He bought sandwich bread, peanut butter, and jelly, and ate in his room most of the time. When we went out to eat as a group, he never ate anything. He saved his money. All he could think about was getting home to buy his boat and start living his life as he had always dreamed about.

I will never forget the night when Jimmy felt like he had saved enough money to buy the boat he wanted. He was elated. I hadn't seen Jimmy this happy in months. All his hard work and sacrifice had paid off, and now his dream was finally within reach.

As I lay in my bed late that night, I could hear Jimmy talking to his girlfriend on the phone through the paper-thin walls that separated our rooms at the motel. He was in tears as he told her about the decisions he had made over the past several months, the boat he was going to buy, and how he was going to find time to start enjoying life. I had a tear in my eye that night as I lay there listening to Jimmy, thinking about my family.

The week before Christmas the company and the union settled their differences, ended the strike, and, within hours, we were on planes returning home. When I got back to Franklin, I immediately took some needed vacation time, and my family and I went home to Alabama to spend the Christmas holidays with our families. However, my thoughts kept going back to Jimmy and the boat I'm sure he was preparing to purchase, getting ready to have the time of his life.

A few days after Christmas, we returned to Franklin so I could go back to work. I looked forward to talking to Jimmy, seeing pictures of his boat, and hearing his plans for his future. But that never happened. Jimmy wasn't standing at the door to greet me as he had done many times before. During the holidays, Jimmy lost his life in a tragic accident.

Jimmy and some of his close friends had a Christmas party on a houseboat at the lake. While dancing on the roof of the boat, Jimmy slipped and hit his head on the side of the boat as he fell into the cold water. Before his friends there that night could get him back onto the boat, he drowned. I was devastated when I heard the news. The news of that day burned into my mind and defined for me how short life really is.

I wish this story had a happy ending. Jimmy was a good friend, and we shared a lot of wonderful and difficult times together. Jimmy, like most of us, let the clutter in his life lure him away from his priorities and kept him from living the life he dreamed about.

Why did I tell you this story? Because, sometimes adults have to be hit between the eyes with a two-by-four before we stop long enough to evaluate our lives to make sure we are living them in the manner that makes us happy. We put off living our lives until some imaginary time in the future, believing that now is not the right time to make necessary changes. As a result, we waste our lives wishing for that someday that may or may not ever get here. That someday can be today if we will only take control of our lives and start focusing on living the simple life we dream about!

Don't be like Jimmy or me. Don't take twenty-seven years, like I did, to find the reason for the emptiness in your life. Don't waste your life hoping and looking for a more appropriate time in the future. Life is too short not to be living your life the way you have imagined it.

Don't let anything cloud your thinking and put off your dreams until sometime in the future. Now is the time to live your dream!

Don't let anything prevent you from taking the first step toward a more meaningful life. Living your life haphazardly will never provide the happiness you are seeking.

Don't let anything prevent you from defining your priorities in life and keeping them close to you. Your priorities are where you find real happiness.

Don't let anything distract you from your financial resources by wasting them on unnecessary wants. Instead, use your financial resources to support your priorities.

Don't let anything steal your valuable time, thinking you have all the time in the world. Time is your most valuable resource, and only you should decide how you spend it.

Don't clutter your life with meaningless relationships, commitments, and stuff. Clutter will take your life away from you if you don't control it.

Don't let anything take your dream of a simpler life or the happiness you are seeking away from you. Living the simple life you dream about is there waiting for you. Reach out and take hold of your new life today!

This is my hope for you. Good luck!

About the Author

Bobby G. Muse Jr. has over thirty years of business experience as a company owner, consultant, and leader. He has held responsible leadership roles in private, government, and Fortune 500 public organizations. Bobby is a graduate of the University of North Alabama in Florence, Alabama, and holds degrees in accounting and business management. In addition, he holds professional certifications in the information management and business continuity fields.

Live The Simple Life You Dream About is Mr. Muse's second book in a series of books to help people simplify their lives and find true happiness through living life more simply. In his first book, *The Building Blocks of Success: Focus On the Fundamentals and Be Successful at Everything You Do*, Bobby simplifies the process of becoming successful to help the reader focus on the seven fundamental elements of success and teaches us how to be successful at everything.

Bobby is married to his high-school sweetheart, Mary, whom he met while sitting across the aisle from her in the fourth grade. They have been happily married for thirty-four years and have two wonderful children, Jonathan and Kristen, who are now embarking on successful careers of their own.

Other Books by Bobby G. Muse Jr.

Being successful at anything in life is not difficult. In fact, it is scary how simple it can be when you fully understand what it takes to be successful. When you break success down into its seven fundamental elements and begin to focus on the things that are really important to being successful, success comes naturally.

The potential for success is present within all of us. Believe it or not, we developed all the tools needed to be successful in every aspect of our life growing up as children. Regrettably, somewhere between childhood and adulthood, many of us forget how to be successful. We make reaching our potential much more difficult than it really is. In the end, the biggest challenge we face in becoming successful is ourselves.

Simplicity is the key to everything in life. Focusing on the fundamentals of success unclutters the process and simplifies our path. The simpler anything is, the easier it is to achieve. Focusing on the fundamentals is the key to being successful at everything you do.

Bobby G. Muse Jr. has over thirty years of experience as a business owner, consultant, and leader and has a passion for helping people follow their dreams. Using his children as an example, he will teach you how to be successful in every part of your life. Bobby is a motivator, encourager, and guide to helping you realize your full potential and live your dream.

Endnotes:

Chapter One: What Does Your Perfect Life Look Like?

[1] Genesis 3: 1–24

[2] Wikipedia, "Decline of the Roman Empire," Wikipedia, http://en.wikipedia.org/w/index.php?title=Decline_of_the_Roman_Empire (accessed September 30, 2013).

[3] Herbert W. Benario, "Nero (54–68 A.D.)," De Imperatoribus Romanis, http://www.roman-emperors.org/nero.htm (accessed September 30, 2013).

[4] Martin Kelly, "Causes of the American Revolution: The Colonial Mind-set and Events That Led to Revolt," About.com American History, http://americanhistory.about.com/od/revolutionarywar/a/amer_revolution.htm?p=1 (accessed September 30, 2013).

[5] Martin Kelly, "Top Five Causes of the Civil War Leading up to Secession and the Civil War," About.com American History, http://americanhistory.about.com/od/civilwarmenu/a/cause_civil_war.htm?p=1 (accessed September 30, 2013).

[6] Guy Gugliotta, "New Estimate Raises Civil War Death Toll" (2012), New York Times, http://www.nytimes.com/2012/04/03/science/civil-war-toll-up-by-20-percent-in-new-estimate.html?pagewanted=all&_r=0 (accessed September 30, 2013).

[7] Martin Kelly, "Top 5 Causes of the Great Depression," About.com American History, http://americanhistory.about.com/od/greatdepression/tp/greatdepression.htm (accessed September 30, 2013).

[8] Kimberly Amadeo, "Black Tuesday," About.com US Economy, http://useconomy.about.com/od/glossary/g/Black_Tuesday.htm (accessed September 30, 2013).

⁹Yuval Rosenberg, "Lessons from 1929," CNN/Money (2004), http://money.cnn.com/2004/10/26/markets/1929crash/ (accessed September 30, 2013).

¹⁰Wikipedia, "Bernard Madoff," Wikipedia, http://en.wikipedia.org/w/index.php?title=Bernard_Madoff (accessed September 30, 2013).

¹¹Grant McCool and Martha Graybow, "Madoff Pleads Guilty, Is Jailed for $65 Billion Fraud," Reuters (2009), http://www.reuters.com/article/2009/03/13/us-madoff-idUSTRE52A5JK20090313 (accessed September 30, 2013).

¹²Valli Sarvani, "10 Major Accounting Scandals," Bizcovering.com http://bizcovering.com/history/10-major-accounting-scandals/ (accessed September 30, 2013).

¹³Richad A. Oppel Jr. and Andrew Ross Sorkin, "Enron's Collapse: The Overview; Enron Collapses as Suitor Cancels Plans for Merger," The New York Times, http://www.nytimes.com/2001/11/29/business/enron-s-collapse-the-overview-enron-collapses-as-suitor-cancels-plans-for-merger.html?pagewanted=print (accessed September 30, 2013).

¹⁴Wikipedia, "Financial Crisis of 2007–08," Wikipedia, http://en.wikipedia.org/wiki/Financial_crisis_of_2007%E2%80%9308 (accessed September 30, 2013).

¹⁵ Nouriel Roubini, Kenneth Rogoff, and Nariman Behravesh, "Three Top Economists Agree 2009 Worst Financial Crisis Since Great Depression; Risks Increase if Right Steps Are Not Taken," Reuters.com (2009), http://www.reuters.com/article/2009/02/27/idUS193520+27-Feb-2009+BW20090227 (accessed September 30, 2013).

¹⁶Martin Neil Baily and Douglas J. Elliott, "The US Financial and Economic Crisis: Where Does It Stand and Where Do We Go from Here?," Brookings.edu (PDF) http://www.brookings.edu/~/media/research/files/papers/2009/6/15%20economic%20crisis%20baily%20elliott/0615_economic_crisis_baily_elliott.pdf (accessed September 30, 2013).

¹⁷Ellen Crean, "Toxic Secret," CBS News 60 Minutes (2009), http://www.cbsnews.com/8301-18560_162-528581.html (accessed September 27, 2013).

¹⁸Michael Grunwald, "Monsanto Hid Decades of Pollution
PCBs Drenched Ala. Town, But No One Was Ever Told," The Washington Post (2002), http://www.commondreams.org/headlines02/0101-02.htm (accessed September 30, 2013).

[19]Marsalis, Diane, "60 Minutes Oil Spill: Accident Could Have Avoided, BP Took Shortcuts (videos)," Houston TV Examiner (2010), http://www.examiner.com/article/60-minutes-oil-spill-accident-could-have-been-avoided-bp-took-shortcuts-videos (accessed September 30, 213).

[20, 21, & 22]Merron, Jeff, "Biggest Sports Gambling Scandals," ESPN (2006) http://sports.espn.go.com/espn/page2/story?page=merron/060207 (accessed September 30, 2013).

[23]ESPN.com News Services, "McGwire Apologizes to La Russa, Selig," ESPN.com (2010), http://m.espn.go.com/mlb/story?storyId=4816607&wjb=&pg=1 (accessed September 30, 2013).

[24]Cork Gaines, "Chart: PEDs Have Destroyed Baseball's List of Career Home Run Leaders," Business Insider (2013), http://www.businessinsider.com/chart-peds-have-destroyed-baseballs-list-of-career-home-run-leaders-2013-8 (accessed September 27, 2013).

[25 & 26]The Trinity Foundation, Inc., "Evangelist Scandals," The Trinity Foundation, http://webspace.webring.com/people/bt/trinityf/scandal.html (accessed September 30, 2013).

[27]Rachel Zoll, "Televangelists Escape Penalty in Senate Inquiry," Associated Press (2011), http://www.nbcnews.com/id/40960871/ns/politics-capitol_hill/t/televangelists-escape-penalty-senate-inquiry/ (accessed September 30, 2013).

[28]Vernon Howard, "You have succeeded in life when all you really want is only what you really need," Brainy Quote, http://www.brainyquote.com/quotes/quotes/v/vernonhowa104699.html#AkYtPZVCWqxficFb.99 (accessed September 30, 2013).

Chapter Four: Live the Simple Life You Dream About

[29]Night at the Museum: Battle of the Smithsonian, dir. By Shawn Levy (2009; Twentieth Century Fox Film Corporation, 2012 dvd)

[30]Betty Crocker, "The Ultimate Chocolate Chip Cookies," General Mills, http://www.bettycrocker.com/recipes/ultimate-chocolate-chip-cookies/77c14e03-d8b0-4844-846d-f19304f61c57 (Accessed October 3, 2013).

Chapter Five: Step Two: Defining Our Priorities

[31]Encarta World English Dictionary, Online Version, s.v. "copy-edit."

[32]Ron Ashkenas, "More Direct Reports Make Life Easier," Harvard Business Review, http://blogs.hbr.org/2012/09/more-direct-reports-make-life/ (accessed October 21, 2013).

Chapter Six: Step Three: Establishing Our Financial Means

[33]Elizabeth W. Dunn, Lara B. Aknin, Michael I. Norton, "Spending Money on Others Promotes Happiness," Science 319, no. 5870 (2008), 1687–1688.

Chapter Seven: Step Four: Establishing Our Time Means

[34]CIA.gov, "The World Factbook," CIA.gov, https://www.cia.gov/library/publications/the-world-factbook/rankorder/2102rank.html (accessed October 21, 2013).

[35]Steven Harper, Fariss-Terry Mousa, "Time and Motion Studies," Oxford Bibliographies (2013), http://www.oxfordbibliographies.com/view/document/obo-9780199846740/obo-9780199846740-0027.xml (accessed October 21, 2013).

[36]Sleep Foundation, "How Much Sleep Do We Really Need?," Sleep Foundation, http://www.sleepfoundation.org/article/how-sleep-works/how-much-sleep-do-we-really-need (accessed October 21, 2013).

Chapter Eight: Step Five: Decluttering Our Lives

[37]Britannica, "Diminishing Returns," Britannica, http://www.britannica.com/EBchecked/topic/163723/diminishing-returns (accessed October 22, 2013).

[38]Investopedia, "Pareto Principle," Investopedia.com, http://www.investopedia.com/terms/p/paretoprinciple.asp (accessed October 22, 2013).

www.ingramcontent.com/pod-product-compliance
Lightning Source LLC
Chambersburg PA
CBHW061648040426
42446CB00010B/1637